SNMP: Monitoring and Security in Network Management

James Relington

DEDICATION

To those who seek knowledge, inspiration, and new perspectives—
may this book be a companion on your journey, a spark for curiosity,
and a reminder that every page turned is a step toward discovery.

AKNOWLEDGEMENTS

I would like to express my deepest gratitude to everyone who contributed to the creation of this book. To my colleagues and mentors, your insights and expertise have been invaluable. A special thank you to my family and friends for their unwavering support and encouragement throughout this journey.

Introduction to SNMP

The Simple Network Management Protocol, more commonly known as SNMP, is a cornerstone of modern network management. Originally developed in the late 1980s, SNMP was designed to provide a simple and effective way for administrators to monitor and manage networked devices. Its simplicity is deceptive, however, as the protocol has proven to be both powerful and highly adaptable, evolving alongside the ever-changing landscape of IT infrastructure. At its core, SNMP enables network administrators to collect information from network devices such as routers, switches, servers, printers, and more, and to modify configurations when needed. This ability to monitor, control, and troubleshoot devices remotely has made SNMP an essential component of enterprise networks, data centers, cloud infrastructures, and even Internet of Things (IoT) environments.

SNMP works based on a client-server model, where the client is called the SNMP manager and the server is the SNMP agent. The SNMP manager is typically a centralized system that sends requests to the SNMP agents residing on network devices. These agents gather device-specific data and respond accordingly. This data includes key operational metrics such as CPU utilization, memory usage, network interface statistics, disk space, and much more. The information is stored in a hierarchical database known as the Management Information Base, or MIB, which acts as a dictionary for the SNMP manager to understand and interpret the data collected from agents. This hierarchical structure allows SNMP to scale effortlessly, accommodating everything from small local networks to vast, globally distributed infrastructures.

From its inception, SNMP was created with ease of implementation in mind, which is one of the reasons why it gained such widespread adoption. Vendors quickly incorporated SNMP agents into their devices, making it a de facto standard in network management. Over time, three major versions of SNMP were developed: SNMPv1, SNMPv2c, and SNMPv3. Each version built upon the foundation of its predecessor, introducing improvements in efficiency, security, and feature sets. SNMPv1 provided the initial framework and basic functionalities but lacked robust security mechanisms. SNMPv2c introduced performance enhancements and bulk data retrieval capabilities but still relied on simple community strings for authentication, which posed significant security risks. SNMPv3 addressed these concerns by implementing user-based security models, encryption, and message integrity, establishing a more secure method of managing network devices in sensitive environments.

Despite the introduction of more modern network management protocols and APIs, SNMP remains deeply embedded in many organizations due to its proven reliability, extensive device support, and compatibility with legacy systems. Its persistence is also tied to its adaptability; SNMP can be integrated with other monitoring tools and frameworks, and its ability to generate traps or alerts in response to critical events makes it valuable for proactive network management. For instance, an SNMP agent can notify the manager if a network interface goes down or if CPU usage exceeds a specified threshold, allowing administrators to take timely action to prevent service disruptions or degradation.

The flexibility of SNMP also lies in its ability to operate in various types of networks, whether traditional on-premises data centers, hybrid cloud environments, or fully virtualized infrastructures. It supports both polling and event-driven models, meaning that network managers can either periodically query devices for updated information or rely on agents to send unsolicited notifications when important events occur. This dual capability helps balance network load and ensures timely visibility into network health and performance.

Another key strength of SNMP is its protocol simplicity, which contributes to its low overhead on network resources. SNMP messages are typically small and lightweight, making them suitable for use in resource-constrained devices such as IoT sensors and embedded systems. Furthermore, SNMP has become synonymous with vendor interoperability. Devices from different manufacturers can be managed through a single SNMP-based monitoring platform, providing a unified view of the network. This cross-vendor compatibility is critical in modern heterogeneous networks where equipment from multiple vendors often coexists.

Despite its many advantages, SNMP is not without challenges. One of its long-standing criticisms has been its early versions' limited focus on security. SNMPv1 and SNMPv2c, which are still in use in many networks today, lack encryption and are vulnerable to eavesdropping and spoofing attacks. This has driven the industry to adopt SNMPv3 in security-conscious environments. However, even SNMPv3 requires careful configuration to maximize its protective features. The shift to encrypted communications, strong authentication, and access control has strengthened SNMP's resilience against modern cyber threats.

The relevance of SNMP in today's network management landscape cannot be overstated. Whether used as a standalone protocol or in conjunction with newer technologies like NetFlow, RESTful APIs, or streaming telemetry, SNMP continues to play a crucial role in providing operational insight and enabling automation. Its widespread use across industries such as telecommunications, finance, healthcare, manufacturing, and government underscores its versatility and reliability.

SNMP has stood the test of time and continues to evolve, adapting to new network paradigms and business requirements. It remains a foundational element in the toolkit of network engineers and IT administrators, helping them maintain visibility, ensure availability, and uphold the performance of the digital infrastructures that power modern organizations.

History and Evolution of SNMP

The story of SNMP begins in the late 1980s, during a time when computer networks were rapidly expanding and becoming critical to business operations and research institutions alike. As the complexity of networks grew, so did the need for a standardized method to monitor and manage devices remotely. Prior to SNMP, network management was largely ad hoc, with each vendor creating proprietary tools and methods that were often incompatible with one another. The lack of a common framework created operational silos, made troubleshooting more difficult, and increased the burden on administrators who had to master multiple systems to gain visibility into their networks. It was against this backdrop that the Simple Network Management Protocol emerged as a practical and scalable solution to unify network management practices.

The origins of SNMP can be traced to the collaborative efforts of several key organizations, including the Internet Engineering Task Force, or IETF. The protocol was initially developed as a temporary fix, a so-called stopgap measure, to address the immediate need for network management tools in the fledgling internet community. The first version, SNMPv1, was formally introduced in 1988 under RFC 1067. Despite its designation as a provisional protocol, SNMPv1 quickly gained traction due to its simplicity, ease of deployment, and the urgent need for a solution that could span multiple types of devices and platforms. Its client-server architecture, based on managers and agents, was intuitive and efficient, allowing administrators to collect and act on network data without extensive overhead or complexity.

SNMPv1 introduced the fundamental building blocks that continue to underpin the protocol today, including the use of Object Identifiers, or OIDs, and the Management Information Base, or MIB. This structure enabled a standardized way to represent and organize information from network devices, regardless of manufacturer. However, as networks continued to grow in size and importance during the 1990s, the limitations of SNMPv1 became increasingly apparent. Chief among these limitations was its lack of robust security. SNMPv1 relied on community strings for authentication, which were often left at default values or transmitted in plain text, leaving networks vulnerable to unauthorized access and potential data tampering.

Recognizing these shortcomings, the IETF began work on an improved version. This led to the development of SNMPv2, which was designed to enhance performance, security, and functionality. Released in 1993, SNMPv2, specifically SNMPv2c, retained the same basic architecture as SNMPv1 but introduced important upgrades such as the GetBulk operation for more efficient data retrieval and new error codes for better diagnostics. However, the attempt to strengthen security through SNMPv2's original party-based security model encountered resistance. The model was deemed too complex and difficult to implement, which led to fragmentation and the parallel use of both SNMPv1 and SNMPv2 in many organizations. Eventually, the community settled on SNMPv2c, a version that preserved the simplicity of SNMPv1's community-based security while benefiting from SNMPv2's performance enhancements. Even so, the critical issue of weak security remained unresolved, prompting ongoing debate within the network management community.

The next major milestone in the evolution of SNMP came with the release of SNMPv3 in 1998 under RFCs 3410 to 3418. SNMPv3 represented a significant step forward, as it introduced a comprehensive security framework to address the vulnerabilities of its predecessors. It featured user-based security models that provided authentication, encryption, and message integrity. These improvements enabled administrators to better safeguard network management communications against eavesdropping, replay attacks, and unauthorized data modifications. By incorporating modern security principles, SNMPv3 gained the trust of industries that operated in highly sensitive environments, such as finance, healthcare, and government sectors. Although SNMPv3 added complexity to the configuration process, its security enhancements were critical for organizations seeking to align with emerging cybersecurity standards and regulatory requirements.

As SNMP matured, it became the backbone of network management in an increasingly connected world. The proliferation of IP networks in both enterprise and service provider environments solidified SNMP's role as a universal protocol for monitoring and control. Network device manufacturers, from giants like Cisco and Juniper to smaller niche players, consistently embedded SNMP agents in their products, further fueling its widespread adoption. SNMP also evolved alongside technological shifts, adapting to the rise of virtualization, data center consolidation, and the emergence of cloud computing. Its compatibility with virtualized switches, routers, and servers enabled administrators to maintain consistent management practices even as underlying infrastructures became more dynamic and abstracted.

The protocol's journey also paralleled the explosion of the Internet of Things, as SNMP was well-suited to monitor and manage the growing ecosystem of connected sensors, devices, and industrial control systems. Its lightweight nature and support for constrained environments made it attractive for IoT deployments, where bandwidth and processing power are often limited. At the same time, the growing sophistication of cyber threats pushed organizations to re-examine SNMP implementations and migrate to SNMPv3 where possible, reinforcing security as a central concern.

Throughout its history, SNMP has faced competition from other protocols and technologies designed to modernize network management. Alternatives such as NetConf, RESTful APIs, and gRPC have gained traction in certain use cases, offering more flexible or programmatic approaches to managing next-generation infrastructures. Yet, SNMP's entrenched position in the industry, coupled with decades of vendor support and operational familiarity, has ensured its continued relevance. Rather than being replaced outright, SNMP is often used in tandem with these newer technologies, forming part of a hybrid management strategy that leverages the strengths of multiple protocols.

Today, SNMP stands as one of the most enduring and influential protocols in the field of network management. Its historical development reflects the broader evolution of computer networks, from early research-driven initiatives to today's mission-critical global infrastructures. The ability of SNMP to adapt and expand across diverse networking environments is a testament to its original design principles and the collaborative efforts of the global internet community. Even as emerging technologies continue to reshape how networks are built and operated, SNMP remains a foundational tool for ensuring the performance, availability, and security of digital systems.

SNMP in Modern Network Management

In the context of modern network management, SNMP continues to serve as a critical tool, despite the emergence of newer technologies and frameworks. As organizations increasingly depend on complex and hybrid IT environments, the demand for reliable, real-time visibility into network performance, availability, and security has never been greater. SNMP plays a pivotal role in meeting this demand by providing a standardized and efficient means of monitoring and controlling devices across diverse infrastructures. From traditional on-premises networks to highly virtualized data centers and expansive cloud environments, SNMP remains a versatile protocol that enables administrators to maintain control over a wide range of devices and services.

Modern networks are no longer limited to a few routers and switches within a corporate LAN. Instead, they encompass thousands of interconnected devices spanning multiple geographies, with data flowing through physical hardware, virtualized resources, and cloud-based services. This complexity requires tools that can aggregate information from disparate systems and present it in a unified, actionable format. SNMP addresses this need by offering a consistent method to query and manage heterogeneous devices, including routers, switches, firewalls, servers, storage arrays, wireless access points, and IoT endpoints. Regardless of the vendor or device type, SNMP provides a common language for monitoring critical parameters such as CPU usage, memory utilization, disk performance, temperature, power supply status, and network traffic patterns.

One of the key reasons SNMP has remained integral to modern network management is its lightweight nature. SNMP messages are small and impose minimal overhead on the network, which is particularly important when monitoring large-scale infrastructures. The protocol supports both polling and event-driven models, giving network operators the flexibility to retrieve data periodically through queries or to receive unsolicited alerts via traps and informs when specific thresholds or conditions are met. This dual capability is vital in contemporary environments where both proactive and reactive management approaches are necessary to ensure optimal service delivery and minimize downtime.

The widespread support for SNMP across the industry has also contributed to its longevity. Virtually every enterprise-grade network device ships with an SNMP agent, making it easy to integrate into existing monitoring platforms. This cross-vendor interoperability is crucial as organizations continue to adopt a mix of legacy and modern equipment. Many IT environments feature a blend of aging hardware and cutting-edge technologies, and SNMP's ability to interface with both ensures a seamless monitoring experience. Even with the rise of APIs and other modern protocols, SNMP remains deeply embedded in network management tools, serving as the foundation for data collection that feeds into performance dashboards, alerting systems, and automated workflows.

Automation and orchestration are key trends in modern IT operations, and SNMP plays an essential supporting role in this evolution. By integrating SNMP into network automation platforms, administrators can create intelligent workflows that respond to network events in real time. For example, when an SNMP trap indicates that a link is down or that a device is approaching a resource threshold, automation tools can trigger predefined actions such as rerouting traffic, provisioning additional virtual machines, or escalating alerts to network operations centers. The ability to feed SNMP-derived metrics directly into orchestration systems enhances operational efficiency and reduces the time needed to diagnose and resolve issues.

In addition to operational benefits, SNMP contributes significantly to security and compliance efforts within modern organizations. SNMPv3's authentication and encryption capabilities help protect sensitive monitoring data from interception and tampering. When configured correctly, SNMPv3 aligns with industry best practices and regulatory requirements related to data integrity and confidentiality. Many organizations also integrate SNMP with security information and event management systems to correlate network anomalies with broader security incidents, thereby enriching threat detection and response capabilities.

The growing prevalence of hybrid and multi-cloud architectures has introduced new challenges for network management, but SNMP has adapted to address these complexities. Cloud service providers often expose SNMP interfaces for monitoring virtualized resources such as cloud-based routers, load balancers, and firewalls. Enterprises leveraging hybrid architectures can use SNMP to bridge the gap between their on-premises infrastructure and cloud-hosted environments, maintaining a holistic view of performance and availability across the entire ecosystem. This visibility is essential for optimizing cloud expenditures, ensuring compliance with service-level agreements, and preventing service disruptions that can negatively impact business operations.

The Internet of Things has further expanded the scope of network management, introducing vast numbers of connected devices that must be monitored and secured. SNMP's lightweight and scalable design makes it well-suited for IoT environments where devices may operate under constraints in terms of processing power and bandwidth. By using SNMP, organizations can efficiently monitor environmental sensors, industrial control systems, and other edge devices to collect telemetry data, detect faults, and maintain system reliability in critical sectors such as manufacturing, transportation, and utilities.

In modern network management, the integration of SNMP with advanced analytics and machine learning tools has opened new possibilities for proactive and predictive monitoring. By feeding SNMP-collected data into analytics engines, organizations can identify patterns and anomalies that might not be immediately apparent through traditional monitoring techniques. Predictive models can use this information to forecast potential failures, recommend optimizations, and enhance decision-making processes. As artificial intelligence becomes more deeply embedded in IT operations, SNMP's role as a reliable data source ensures that machine learning algorithms are fueled with accurate and timely information.

While SNMP may no longer be the only protocol available to network administrators, it continues to serve as a critical layer within the broader network management stack. It complements modern APIs and telemetry solutions by providing quick and easy access to standardized metrics, making it an invaluable resource for teams responsible for maintaining the health and performance of today's complex digital infrastructures. SNMP's ability to scale from small branch offices to global enterprise networks, combined with its seamless integration into traditional and modern monitoring platforms, ensures that it remains a fundamental component of contemporary network management strategies.

The ongoing evolution of IT environments has not diminished the relevance of SNMP; rather, it has highlighted the importance of having a stable and proven protocol at the core of network visibility and control. As organizations continue to push the boundaries of technology adoption, SNMP remains a trusted ally in the pursuit of operational excellence and network resilience.

The SNMP Protocol Suite

The SNMP protocol suite is a collection of components, mechanisms, and specifications that work together to enable the monitoring and management of network devices across diverse environments. While SNMP is often spoken of as a singular protocol, it is, in reality, a layered system composed of multiple interconnected elements, each playing a vital role in ensuring effective communication between network management systems and the devices they oversee. Understanding the SNMP protocol suite requires a deep dive into how these components interact to facilitate the seamless exchange of management information across both small-scale and enterprise-level networks.

At the heart of the SNMP protocol suite is the protocol itself, which operates at the application layer of the OSI model. It is built on top of the User Datagram Protocol, or UDP, a lightweight transport protocol that offers connectionless communication between SNMP managers and SNMP agents. UDP's minimal overhead makes it well-suited for the frequent, real-time data exchanges required in network management. SNMP typically operates over UDP port 161 for general messages such as Get, Set, GetNext, and GetBulk requests, while UDP port 162 is reserved for traps and informs, which are unsolicited notifications sent from agents to managers. The choice of UDP reflects a design philosophy centered on efficiency and speed, enabling SNMP to perform well in environments where bandwidth and processing resources may be limited.

Beyond the transport layer, the SNMP protocol suite defines a set of fundamental operations that enable network managers to interact with agents. These operations include the Get request, used to retrieve the value of specific variables from a device's Management Information Base, or MIB; the Set request, which allows a manager to modify configuration parameters on the device; the GetNext and GetBulk requests, which facilitate the retrieval of multiple pieces of information, streamlining the process of walking through a device's MIB hierarchy; and the Trap and Inform messages, which serve as proactive notifications from agents when predefined events or thresholds are triggered. Each of these operations plays a unique role in network management, supporting tasks such as performance monitoring, fault detection, capacity planning, and configuration management.

The Management Information Base is another critical component of the SNMP protocol suite. It is a virtual database containing structured information about the device, defined using a hierarchical system of Object Identifiers, or OIDs. Each OID corresponds to a specific variable that represents a measurable characteristic of the device, such as interface status, CPU load, memory usage, or temperature. The structure of the MIB follows a tree-like organization, with each level of the tree representing increasingly specific categories of information. The MIB is standardized through the Structure of Management Information, or SMI, which dictates how objects are named, typed, and encoded. This standardization ensures that SNMP can be universally understood and implemented across equipment from different vendors.

Central to the SNMP protocol suite are the distinct versions that have been developed over time, each bringing enhancements and refinements to the protocol's capabilities. SNMPv1 laid the groundwork with a straightforward, community-string-based authentication model and basic message types. It was effective but limited in its security and scalability. SNMPv2 introduced improvements such as the GetBulk request, allowing for more efficient data retrieval, especially in larger environments with extensive MIBs. However, the early security enhancements in SNMPv2 were considered too complex, leading to the adoption of SNMPv2c, which retained the simplicity of community strings while incorporating SNMPv2's functional benefits. The most secure iteration, SNMPv3, introduced robust features such as user-based authentication, encryption through privacy protocols, and message integrity checks, addressing the critical need for securing network management communications against modern cyber threats.

Another essential aspect of the SNMP protocol suite is its encoding and data representation mechanisms. SNMP messages are encoded using the Abstract Syntax Notation One, or ASN.1, and the Basic Encoding Rules, or BER. ASN.1 provides a formal notation for describing data structures that can be exchanged across heterogeneous systems, while BER defines how these structures are serialized for transmission over a network. This approach ensures platform-independent data exchange, allowing SNMP managers and agents running on different operating systems and hardware platforms to communicate seamlessly. The efficiency and reliability of ASN.1 and BER contribute to the protocol's ability to operate in varied environments, from high-performance data centers to remote field installations with limited resources.

SNMP's flexibility is further demonstrated by its support for both polling-based and event-driven network management paradigms. In polling mode, the SNMP manager periodically sends Get or GetBulk requests to gather information from agents at regular intervals, creating a historical record of network performance and health metrics. In contrast, event-driven management relies on traps and informs, which are sent asynchronously by agents to notify managers of significant events, such as hardware failures, threshold breaches, or security incidents. This combination allows network administrators to tailor SNMP's use to the specific needs of their organization, balancing network traffic efficiency with timely incident detection.

Over the years, the SNMP protocol suite has been extended through proprietary and custom MIBs, enabling organizations to monitor and manage specialized equipment and services beyond the standard definitions provided by the IETF. Vendors often develop their own MIB modules to expose unique features and metrics of their devices, allowing network administrators to access deeper insights and exert finer control over their infrastructure. The extensibility of the MIB system has contributed to SNMP's continued relevance, making it a highly adaptable protocol that can address a wide variety of use cases.

While SNMP is often discussed alongside other management frameworks, such as Remote Monitoring (RMON) and NetConf, it continues to serve as a foundational layer within the broader network management ecosystem. Many modern tools and platforms leverage SNMP alongside newer technologies, using its well-established suite of capabilities as a trusted mechanism for real-time device monitoring, alerting, and control. As networks become increasingly dynamic, driven by trends like software-defined networking, cloud-native architectures, and edge computing, the SNMP protocol suite provides a stable and familiar interface to ensure continuity and visibility across these evolving landscapes.

The enduring strength of the SNMP protocol suite lies in its modularity and standardization, which have enabled it to adapt to shifting technological paradigms while maintaining interoperability and efficiency. As organizations continue to seek comprehensive solutions for managing increasingly complex and distributed environments, SNMP's role as a cornerstone of network management infrastructure remains firmly established.

SNMP Architecture and Components

The architecture of SNMP is based on a simple but highly effective model that allows for efficient communication between devices and management systems within a network. This architecture is composed of three primary components: SNMP managers, SNMP agents, and the Management Information Base, commonly referred to as the MIB. Together, these elements form a distributed system designed to monitor, control, and manage devices across a variety of network environments, from small office networks to vast, multi-site enterprise infrastructures. Despite its relatively simple design, the SNMP architecture is capable of supporting complex tasks, making it a cornerstone of network management.

At the core of SNMP architecture is the SNMP manager, which acts as the centralized control point in the system. The manager is typically implemented as part of a Network Management System, or NMS, running on a server that continuously polls devices or listens for notifications sent by those devices. The manager's primary role is to send requests to SNMP agents installed on network devices, retrieve data from them, and sometimes modify certain operational parameters. The SNMP manager is also responsible for processing traps and informs, which are messages sent by agents when specific events occur, such as link failures or threshold breaches. The information collected by the manager is used to monitor device status, analyze performance trends, identify potential problems, and automate responses when necessary.

The SNMP agent is the counterpart to the manager. Installed on network devices such as routers, switches, servers, printers, and even IoT devices, the agent functions as the local representative of the device's operational data. It gathers information from the hardware and operating system and makes it available to the SNMP manager via standardized methods. The agent collects data on key metrics such as interface status, CPU usage, memory utilization, disk space availability, and environmental factors like temperature and power supply condition. This information is made accessible to the manager through the Management Information Base, a hierarchical database maintained by each agent. In addition to responding to queries from the manager, the agent can also initiate communication in the form of traps and informs, alerting the manager to events that require immediate attention.

The Management Information Base serves as a critical link between the manager and the agent. It is a virtual database that organizes network management data in a hierarchical structure defined by Object Identifiers, or OIDs. Each OID represents a unique object, which could be a hardware parameter, configuration setting, or performance statistic. The hierarchical structure is tree-like, beginning with a root that branches out into categories such as system, interfaces, transmission, and specific vendor extensions. This structure ensures that SNMP managers can query agents in a consistent and organized manner, regardless of device type or manufacturer. The MIB is defined using the Structure of Management Information, or SMI, which establishes the rules for naming objects, defining data types, and encoding information for transmission. Standard MIBs, such as MIB-II defined by the IETF, provide universally recognized objects for common device attributes, while vendors often create custom MIBs to expose proprietary features of their equipment.

A key characteristic of SNMP's architecture is its reliance on a simple set of operations that allow managers and agents to interact. These include Get, Set, GetNext, GetBulk, Trap, and Inform operations. The Get operation allows the manager to retrieve the value of a specific object from an agent's MIB. The Set operation enables the manager to modify the value of a writable object on the agent, which can be used for remote configuration changes. The GetNext and GetBulk operations allow for efficient traversal of the MIB tree, making it possible to retrieve large sets of related data with fewer requests. Traps and Informs are unsolicited messages that agents send to managers to report significant events. While traps are sent without expecting an acknowledgment, informs are designed to ensure reliable delivery by requiring a confirmation from the manager.

The SNMP architecture is built on top of the User Datagram Protocol, or UDP, at the transport layer. This choice was made to prioritize speed and efficiency, as UDP's connectionless nature allows SNMP messages to be transmitted with minimal overhead. SNMP typically operates over UDP port 161 for general communication between managers and agents and port 162 for traps and informs. While the use of UDP introduces the possibility of lost messages, SNMP compensates for this by relying on periodic polling and the redundancy of receiving unsolicited notifications from agents.

Security within SNMP architecture has evolved significantly across its versions. In SNMPv1 and SNMPv2c, security was limited to community strings, which served as simple passwords included in SNMP messages. While this provided basic access control, the lack of encryption left SNMPv1 and SNMPv2c communications vulnerable to interception and spoofing. The introduction of SNMPv3 addressed these shortcomings by incorporating a comprehensive security model that includes authentication, encryption, and message integrity. SNMPv3 allows administrators to define users with specific roles and access privileges, enabling fine-grained control over which objects can be read or modified by different users. The protocol also supports encryption through privacy protocols, safeguarding sensitive data from eavesdropping as it traverses the network.

Another component of SNMP architecture worth highlighting is the extensibility provided by the use of custom MIBs. Vendors can design MIB modules tailored to the unique capabilities of their devices, allowing administrators to monitor proprietary features not covered by standard MIB definitions. This flexibility has made SNMP highly adaptable and suitable for managing both generic and specialized network equipment. Organizations can leverage custom MIBs to monitor advanced features such as hardware health sensors, application-specific counters, or custom service-level metrics. This extensibility has been key to SNMP's success in heterogeneous environments where equipment from multiple manufacturers must be managed through a single monitoring platform.

SNMP's distributed architecture also makes it inherently scalable. In large-scale networks, multiple SNMP managers can be deployed to handle different segments of the infrastructure, distributing the workload and providing redundancy in case of manager failure. Similarly, agents can be installed on virtually any device capable of running an SNMP daemon or service, from high-end core routers to low-powered edge devices. This scalability enables SNMP to support environments ranging from small office LANs to globally distributed wide-area networks.

By combining simplicity, extensibility, and efficiency, SNMP's architecture has proven to be both resilient and adaptable to changing network management needs. The fundamental relationship between managers, agents, and MIBs remains unchanged, but the ways in which they are implemented and secured have evolved to meet modern demands. Whether deployed in a traditional data center, a virtualized cloud infrastructure, or a distributed IoT deployment, SNMP continues to provide the foundational architecture needed for effective and scalable network management.

Understanding SNMP Managers and Agents

At the core of the Simple Network Management Protocol (SNMP) lie two critical entities: the SNMP manager and the SNMP agent. These components form the essential communication bridge that enables network monitoring and control in SNMP-based systems. Their relationship is based on a client-server model, where the manager acts as the client and the agent as the server. This relationship allows administrators to gather and modify information on devices distributed across local or geographically dispersed networks. Together, SNMP managers and agents provide the foundation for monitoring the health, performance, and availability of network devices and services.

The SNMP manager is the centralized brain of the SNMP system. It is responsible for initiating communication with SNMP agents and collecting data from them. The manager is typically deployed as part of a Network Management System (NMS) running on a dedicated server or virtual machine. This centralized system monitors all devices within its scope, issues requests, receives responses, processes alerts, and provides administrators with a consolidated view of the network. The manager performs several tasks, including polling devices to gather status and performance metrics, issuing configuration changes when needed, and receiving unsolicited notifications in the form of traps or informs. The manager's role is crucial because it correlates and analyzes data from multiple agents to detect network anomalies, identify performance bottlenecks, and generate actionable insights.

The SNMP manager also serves as the interface between the network infrastructure and the human operator. It often provides graphical dashboards, reporting capabilities, and alerting mechanisms to visualize network health and trends. These tools help administrators make informed decisions and take corrective actions in response to detected issues. In larger environments, SNMP managers can be part of more sophisticated systems that integrate SNMP data into broader IT operations frameworks, feeding into security information and event management systems or automation platforms that drive network orchestration tasks.

The SNMP agent, on the other hand, resides on the network device itself. It is a software component, often embedded in the firmware of devices such as routers, switches, firewalls, printers, servers, and even IoT endpoints. The agent's primary function is to collect and store information about the local device and respond to requests from the SNMP manager. This data includes device-specific information, such as interface statistics, CPU and memory usage, disk utilization, fan and temperature status, and operational errors. The agent accesses this information from the device's operating system or hardware sensors and makes it available via the Management Information Base (MIB), which organizes the data in a hierarchical format.

Agents are not passive participants in the SNMP model. While they respond to requests from managers, they also have the capability to initiate communication through traps and informs. These unsolicited messages are sent to the manager when significant events occur on the device, such as a failed power supply, a dropped network link, or a security breach. This proactive behavior ensures that critical issues can be detected and acted upon immediately, rather than waiting for the next polling cycle by the manager. Traps are sent without expecting acknowledgment, while informs require confirmation from the manager, ensuring more reliable delivery.

The interaction between managers and agents is carried out using SNMP protocol operations, including Get, Set, GetNext, GetBulk, Trap, and Inform messages. The Get request is used by the manager to retrieve the current value of a specific OID (Object Identifier) from an agent's MIB. The Set request allows the manager to modify the value of a writable object, thereby enabling remote configuration changes. The GetNext and GetBulk requests facilitate walking through or retrieving large sections of the MIB tree efficiently. While the GetNext operation retrieves the next object in the MIB hierarchy, the GetBulk operation is optimized for larger data retrievals, reducing the number of requests required for comprehensive monitoring.

A defining characteristic of the manager-agent relationship is its scalability. A single manager can oversee hundreds or thousands of agents, depending on the size and complexity of the network. Each agent operates independently, focusing solely on its own device and reporting its data to the manager. This distributed nature ensures that device monitoring does not overwhelm any single component within the SNMP ecosystem. Moreover, agents typically require minimal processing power and memory, making them suitable for deployment on resource-constrained devices, including embedded systems and IoT devices.

While the manager-agent architecture is relatively straightforward, its implementation varies depending on the version of SNMP in use. SNMPv1 and SNMPv2c employ community strings for basic authentication. These community strings act like shared passwords, controlling access to the MIB data exposed by the agent. However, the simplicity of this model also poses security risks, as community strings are transmitted in clear text and can be intercepted by malicious actors. SNMPv3 enhances this relationship by adding secure user authentication, encryption of messages, and message integrity checks, thereby protecting the manager-agent communication from eavesdropping, spoofing, and tampering.

The reliability of SNMP manager-agent communication is influenced by the underlying transport protocol, which is typically the User Datagram Protocol (UDP). UDP is favored for its low overhead and speed, but it is connectionless, meaning there are no guarantees of message delivery. To mitigate this limitation, SNMP managers often implement retries and timeouts to handle lost or delayed messages. Additionally, event-driven notifications through traps and informs help ensure that critical alerts are received promptly, even if periodic polling misses transient events.

Modern SNMP managers and agents are also designed to integrate into broader management frameworks that encompass multiple network monitoring and automation protocols. Many Network Management Systems leverage SNMP data alongside syslog messages, NetFlow records, and RESTful API feeds to provide a holistic view of the network. SNMP managers often serve as the data collection point for these multiple streams, correlating information to create comprehensive health and performance reports. In hybrid cloud and multi-cloud environments, SNMP managers continue to play a crucial role by gathering telemetry from on-premises devices and cloud-based virtual instances through SNMP-enabled services.

The relationship between SNMP managers and agents is symbiotic. The manager relies on the agent to deliver accurate, real-time data from the network's edge, while the agent depends on the manager to analyze and act on that data in a centralized and coordinated manner. This relationship enables network administrators to monitor the status of thousands of devices from a single control point, reducing operational complexity and improving network resilience. Whether in legacy systems or modern, dynamic cloud infrastructures, the manager-agent architecture of SNMP continues to provide the essential backbone for effective and scalable network management.

Management Information Base (MIB) Overview

The Management Information Base, or MIB, is a fundamental element of the SNMP ecosystem, acting as the structured framework through which network devices present their operational data to SNMP managers. Without the MIB, the communication between SNMP managers and agents would be disorganized and unintelligible. The MIB provides the essential structure and common language that allow the SNMP manager to understand the data provided by an SNMP agent and take appropriate action based on that information. It is the organized dictionary that defines all the manageable objects within a network device and forms the core data repository that SNMP agents reference to report metrics and system states.

The MIB is built as a hierarchical database where each item, known as a managed object, is identified by a unique Object Identifier, or OID. This hierarchy is similar in concept to a directory tree in a file system, starting from a root node and branching into multiple sub-nodes that categorize data into logical groupings. Each node in this structure is assigned a number, and the sequence of numbers forms the full OID, which uniquely identifies a particular object. For example, an OID might look like a series of numbers separated by dots, such as 1.3.6.1.2.1.1.5. This identifier leads the manager to a specific data point, such as the system name of a device. The numerical structure of OIDs ensures that they are globally unique, eliminating any ambiguity when accessing or modifying device parameters.

The root of the MIB tree is administered by the International Organization for Standardization (ISO) and branches into several main nodes, including organizations like ISO, ITU-T, and joint-ISO-ITU-T. Within this global namespace, certain branches are dedicated to standard MIB definitions, such as the Internet branch, which leads to the widely used MIB-II defined under the 1.3.6.1.2.1 subtree. MIB-II is the most common set of managed objects and includes general-purpose data applicable to nearly all network devices, including system descriptions, interface statistics, IP routing tables, and TCP/UDP connection information. MIB-II serves as the baseline for SNMP monitoring and has been implemented across an enormous range of hardware and software platforms, ensuring interoperability across multi-vendor environments.

The structure of the MIB is governed by the Structure of Management Information (SMI), which establishes the rules for how objects are named, defined, and formatted. The SMI specifies that each object in the MIB must have a name, a unique OID, a data type, and a description of its functionality. Data types can range from simple integers and strings to more complex structures such as tables and sequences. The SMI standard also defines how these data types are encoded using the Abstract Syntax Notation One (ASN.1) and the Basic Encoding Rules (BER), which facilitate platform-independent data exchange between SNMP managers and agents.

In addition to standard MIB modules like MIB-II, vendors frequently develop custom MIBs to expose proprietary features and device-specific metrics not covered by public standards. These custom MIBs are extensions to the standard MIB tree, typically branching under enterprise-specific subtrees such as 1.3.6.1.4.1, which is reserved for private organizations. Under this enterprise branch, companies like Cisco, Juniper, Hewlett Packard, and others define their unique MIB modules to allow network administrators to monitor specialized features such as chassis status, proprietary hardware sensors, or custom traffic policies. This ability to create vendor-specific MIBs is one of the reasons why SNMP remains highly adaptable and scalable in heterogeneous network environments.

The MIB's tabular structures are particularly significant in representing complex sets of related data, such as interface tables, routing tables, and ARP caches. These tables are composed of rows and columns, where each row represents an instance of a particular resource and each column represents an attribute of that resource. For instance, the Interface Table (ifTable) is a common MIB table where each row corresponds to a physical or logical interface on the device, and each column holds information such as interface speed, operational status, or input and output octet counters. SNMP managers use operations like GetNext or GetBulk to traverse these tables efficiently, gathering detailed information about multiple resources with fewer requests.

Another critical aspect of the MIB is that it abstracts the complexities of the underlying device. From the perspective of the SNMP manager, it does not need to understand the internal workings of the device hardware or software. Instead, it simply queries the MIB to retrieve the necessary data or to instruct the device to take a certain action. This abstraction simplifies network management, as administrators can use the same set of SNMP tools and commands to monitor and configure devices from various manufacturers, provided they adhere to the MIB definitions.

MIBs also play a pivotal role in the generation of SNMP traps and informs. When a predefined event occurs, such as an interface going down or a system overheating, the SNMP agent references the MIB to determine which OID should be included in the trap message sent to the manager. This OID identifies the nature of the event and provides context to the manager, allowing it to process the alert and trigger any necessary response actions, such as sending notifications to administrators or executing automated remediation workflows.

To effectively leverage the power of the MIB, network administrators and engineers often rely on MIB browsers or SNMP management platforms that can parse and present MIB objects in a human-readable format. These tools simplify the process of navigating the MIB tree, identifying relevant OIDs, and interpreting the data collected from SNMP agents. They also facilitate troubleshooting by allowing administrators to inspect live values of MIB objects directly from monitored devices.

The MIB is not static; it evolves over time. As technology advances and new networking paradigms emerge, the IETF and other standardization bodies continue to publish new MIB modules to address the changing needs of the industry. Similarly, vendors update their custom MIBs to reflect enhancements in their hardware and software offerings. This ongoing development ensures that SNMP remains a relevant and effective protocol for managing both legacy and cutting-edge network infrastructures.

The Management Information Base serves as the essential backbone that allows SNMP managers and agents to communicate efficiently and effectively. By providing a structured and extensible framework for representing network device information, the MIB transforms raw data into actionable intelligence, enabling administrators to monitor performance, detect faults, optimize configurations, and maintain the health and availability of critical network systems.

Structure of Management Information (SMI)

The Structure of Management Information, commonly known as SMI, is one of the essential foundations that supports the SNMP protocol. It defines the rules and guidelines for how data is organized, named, and typed within the SNMP Management Information Base (MIB). Without the SMI, the MIB would lack the consistency and structure required for interoperability among the vast array of devices and systems that SNMP manages. The SMI is not a single document or standard but rather a framework of specifications that standardizes how managed objects are described and how they interact within the SNMP environment. It is critical to understanding how SNMP agents present data and how SNMP managers interpret that data.

The SMI exists to ensure that SNMP can operate seamlessly in multi-vendor environments, where devices from different manufacturers must be managed by the same network management systems. To achieve this level of consistency, the SMI specifies three core elements: the naming of objects, their syntax, and their encoding. These elements combine to define how objects within the MIB are represented and how SNMP messages carry those objects across a network.

Naming in SMI is achieved through the use of Object Identifiers, or OIDs. Each managed object within a device's MIB is assigned a globally unique OID, which is a sequence of numbers organized hierarchically, similar to a path in a directory tree. For example, the OID 1.3.6.1.2.1.1.1 refers to the system description of a network device, a common object found in the standard MIB-II module. Each level of the OID hierarchy corresponds to an organizational or functional level, starting from an international root maintained by standards bodies such as ISO and branching out to increasingly specific objects defined by standard organizations or individual vendors. This hierarchical structure enables network management systems to navigate the MIB tree logically and retrieve specific data points from SNMP agents.

The syntax component of SMI defines the data types that can be used to describe the attributes of managed objects. These data types are based on Abstract Syntax Notation One (ASN.1), a standard interface description language used widely in telecommunications and computer networking. The SMI defines several standard ASN.1 data types, such as INTEGER, OCTET STRING, OBJECT IDENTIFIER, NULL, and SEQUENCE. Each managed object is assigned one of these types, which tells the SNMP manager how to interpret the value retrieved from the agent. For instance, an INTEGER type might represent a numeric counter or status code, while an OCTET STRING could represent textual information like a device name or location.

In addition to these base types, the SMI introduces a set of derived or application-specific types that provide greater semantic meaning. Examples include Counter32, Gauge32, TimeTicks, and IpAddress. The

Counter32 type is used for counters that increase until they reach their maximum value and then reset to zero. Gauge32 represents a numeric value that can increase or decrease, such as the current temperature or memory utilization. TimeTicks measures time in hundredths of a second since a device was last initialized, making it useful for uptime metrics. IpAddress is used to represent IP addresses in a standardized, four-octet format. These application-specific types enhance the expressiveness of MIB objects and help ensure that SNMP managers can present the retrieved data meaningfully.

The third key element of SMI is the encoding rules, which specify how objects are serialized for transmission between SNMP agents and managers. The SMI mandates the use of Basic Encoding Rules (BER), a set of guidelines for encoding ASN.1 data structures into a binary format. BER ensures that SNMP messages can be reliably interpreted regardless of differences in hardware, operating systems, or software implementations. Each data structure is encoded as a triplet consisting of a type identifier, a length field, and the value itself. This uniform encoding mechanism facilitates interoperability between SNMP managers and agents across different vendors and platforms.

The SMI has undergone several revisions throughout its history, reflecting the evolving needs of network management and SNMP's maturation as a protocol. The initial specification, known as SMIv1, was introduced alongside SNMPv1 and provided the basic naming, syntax, and encoding rules necessary for early SNMP implementations. As SNMP networks became more complex and the demands on monitoring systems increased, SMIv2 was introduced to expand and refine the original model. SMIv2 added new data types, such as Counter64 for high-capacity counters and more flexible table structures for organizing related objects.

SMIv2 also introduced the concept of MODULE-IDENTITY, which groups related managed objects into MIB modules with metadata such as the module's name, last update time, organization, and contact information. This feature makes it easier for administrators and developers to understand the scope and purpose of a given MIB module, facilitating the development of custom monitoring and management tools. Another important addition in SMIv2 is the TEXTUAL-CONVENTION construct, which allows MIB authors to define custom data representations with descriptive naming and formatting rules. For example, a textual convention might define a new type for representing temperature values with explicit units such as degrees Celsius, improving the readability and usability of the MIB.

While SMIv2 is widely adopted and serves as the basis for most modern MIB modules, both SMIv1 and SMIv2 definitions remain in use, ensuring backward compatibility with legacy SNMP implementations. This dual support is critical in large enterprises where older equipment may still be in operation alongside newer devices, all of which must be managed by the same network management system.

In real-world network environments, the SMI serves as the backbone for how SNMP managers interpret and present data. When an administrator queries a device for its system uptime, for example, the SNMP manager references the OID associated with the system uptime object, checks its syntax as defined by the SMI, decodes the BER-encoded data received from the agent, and displays the value in a human-readable format. The administrator may never interact directly with the SMI itself, but the structure and consistency it provides make it possible for the SNMP manager to function reliably and accurately.

The SMI is not simply a technical requirement; it also represents a philosophy of standardization and interoperability. It enables different manufacturers to create devices that can be integrated into diverse network environments without forcing administrators to learn proprietary management methods for each device type. Instead, network operators can rely on the standardized naming, typing, and encoding provided by the SMI to manage thousands of devices through a unified interface. This has made SNMP, and by extension the SMI, one of the most successful frameworks in the history of network management.

The SMI's role in shaping SNMP-based network management is pivotal. It ensures that the complex information collected from routers, switches, servers, and other devices can be efficiently and accurately conveyed across networks of varying sizes and configurations. As the landscape of IT continues to evolve with cloud computing, IoT, and software-defined infrastructures, the principles established by the SMI continue to provide a solid foundation for the structured and consistent representation of management information.

SNMP Versions: v1, v2c, and v3

The evolution of SNMP has been marked by three principal versions: SNMPv1, SNMPv2c, and SNMPv3. Each version reflects the growing needs of network management as infrastructures became more complex, and as security concerns began to take a more prominent role in operational strategies. While the core functionality of SNMP has remained consistent throughout these versions, focusing on monitoring and managing network devices through managers and agents, each iteration introduced significant changes that enhanced the protocol's efficiency, scalability, and security.

SNMPv1, introduced in 1988, was the first implementation of the protocol and laid the groundwork for standardized network management. It was developed at a time when the internet was still in its early stages, and the need for a simple yet effective monitoring protocol was urgent. SNMPv1 provided the essential operations of Get, Set, GetNext, and Trap, allowing network managers to retrieve information, make configuration changes, and receive alerts from devices. The architecture of SNMPv1 was based on a manager-agent model and used community strings for basic authentication. These community strings acted like passwords that determined whether a manager could read or write to an agent's MIB. Typically, network devices were configured with a public community string for read-only access and a private community string for write access. Despite being effective in simple network environments, SNMPv1 suffered from significant limitations, particularly its lack of security features. Community strings were sent in plaintext, making them vulnerable to interception. Additionally, SNMPv1 used a limited set of data types and lacked the ability to efficiently gather large datasets, which became problematic as networks expanded in size and complexity.

Recognizing these shortcomings, the IETF developed SNMPv2 in the early 1990s. SNMPv2 introduced several important improvements over SNMPv1, most notably the addition of the GetBulk operation, which allowed managers to retrieve large amounts of data with fewer requests. This enhancement was especially beneficial when traversing MIB tables, such as interface or routing tables, as it significantly reduced the amount of network traffic generated during polling operations. SNMPv2 also expanded the set of data types, including Counter64, which provided 64-bit counters suitable for high-speed network interfaces. However, the security model proposed in the initial SNMPv2 specification was complex and difficult to implement. This model, known as the party-based security system, aimed to introduce fine-grained access controls and cryptographic security but failed to gain widespread acceptance due to its complexity.

In response to this implementation challenge, a simpler variant called SNMPv2c was introduced. SNMPv2c retained the enhanced functionality of SNMPv2, including GetBulk and the expanded data types, while reverting to the community-based security model of SNMPv1. This compromise allowed organizations to benefit from SNMPv2's performance and scalability improvements without the complexities of the new security model. However, SNMPv2c still transmitted community strings in plaintext, leaving security as an unresolved issue. Despite this, SNMPv2c gained wide adoption due to its simplicity and backward compatibility with SNMPv1. Many organizations deployed SNMPv2c in parallel with SNMPv1, gradually migrating devices to SNMPv2c as they upgraded network equipment.

The most significant leap in SNMP's evolution came with the release of SNMPv3 in 1998. SNMPv3 addressed the critical security weaknesses present in SNMPv1 and SNMPv2c by introducing a comprehensive security framework that incorporated authentication, encryption, and message integrity. The SNMPv3 User-based Security Model (USM) enabled administrators to create user accounts with defined access privileges, securing SNMP communications through authentication protocols such as MD5 or SHA for verifying message origin and integrity. SNMPv3 also supported encryption using privacy protocols like DES to protect data from eavesdropping as it traveled across the network. These enhancements made SNMPv3 suitable for deployment in sensitive and highly regulated environments, including financial services, healthcare, and government networks.

Beyond security, SNMPv3 introduced other architectural improvements. The View-based Access Control Model (VACM) provided administrators with granular control over which parts of the MIB each user could access. This allowed organizations to define views that exposed only specific OIDs to certain users or management systems, minimizing the risk of unauthorized access or accidental configuration changes. SNMPv3 also introduced an improved error-reporting mechanism, offering clearer diagnostic information when operations failed or encountered issues. Despite its clear advantages, the adoption of SNMPv3 was slower than expected in some sectors due to the increased complexity involved in configuring secure SNMPv3 agents and managers.

While SNMPv3 is now widely recognized as the most secure and robust version of the protocol, many organizations still operate mixed environments where SNMPv1, SNMPv2c, and SNMPv3 coexist. This is often due to legacy equipment that only supports older versions of SNMP, or due to operational inertia where SNMPv2c's simplicity and ease of deployment continue to be favored for less critical network segments. Modern SNMP managers are typically designed to support all three versions simultaneously, dynamically selecting the appropriate protocol based on the capabilities and configuration of each monitored device.

The differences between these versions go beyond security. For example, SNMPv3's ability to manage user-based authentication and fine-grained access controls provides a level of operational control not achievable in SNMPv1 and SNMPv2c environments. SNMPv3 also aligns with contemporary best practices for securing network management protocols, supporting compliance with regulatory frameworks that require encryption and strong authentication.

Despite the emergence of alternative network management protocols and APIs, such as NETCONF and RESTful interfaces, SNMPv3 continues to be a reliable and widely used standard. It offers a balanced approach to network monitoring by combining the lightweight, low-bandwidth characteristics inherited from earlier versions with robust security mechanisms required by modern enterprises. SNMPv1 and SNMPv2c, while still present in legacy systems, are increasingly being phased out in environments where security is a primary concern.

The progression from SNMPv1 to SNMPv3 highlights the broader trend in network management toward greater scalability, performance optimization, and most critically, security hardening. The lessons learned through each version of SNMP reflect the growing recognition that while operational simplicity is important, protecting network management traffic from compromise is essential in an era where cyber threats are more sophisticated and persistent than ever before.

Understanding these three versions is essential for network administrators and engineers tasked with maintaining visibility across diverse infrastructures. Whether overseeing small office networks or large enterprise and cloud-based environments, selecting the appropriate SNMP version and configuring it correctly can have a significant impact on both operational efficiency and security posture. Each version of SNMP has played a key role in the protocol's evolution and continues to influence how organizations approach network management today.

SNMP Operations: Get, Set, GetNext, and Trap

The power of SNMP lies not only in its architecture and extensible MIB framework but also in the fundamental operations that enable communication between SNMP managers and agents. These operations form the operational backbone of the protocol, allowing administrators to retrieve information, modify configurations, and receive notifications from devices in real time. Among the core SNMP operations are Get, Set, GetNext, and Trap. Each of these plays a distinct and crucial role in facilitating efficient network management and ensuring that devices across the infrastructure remain visible, controllable, and responsive to both routine and critical events.

The Get operation is perhaps the most widely used and straightforward of all SNMP commands. When a manager sends a Get request to an SNMP agent, it is querying for the current value of a specific object within the agent's Management Information Base. This operation is used primarily for monitoring and information-gathering purposes.

For example, a manager might issue a Get request to retrieve the CPU utilization of a router or the number of packets received on a particular network interface. The agent responds with the value of the requested object, allowing the manager to collect and display this information on dashboards, reports, or alerting systems. The Get operation can target single objects or multiple objects in a single transaction, depending on the capabilities of the SNMP manager. It is an essential part of routine network monitoring and is typically used in periodic polling to ensure that network performance and device health are within acceptable parameters.

The Set operation serves a different but equally important purpose. While Get retrieves information, Set modifies it. Using the Set operation, an SNMP manager can instruct an SNMP agent to change the value of a writable object within its MIB. This allows administrators to remotely alter configurations, enabling automated or manual adjustments without physically accessing the device. For instance, a Set request might be used to reset an interface, adjust traffic thresholds, or reconfigure system settings on the fly. The power of the Set operation lies in its ability to enable centralized control over distributed devices. However, its use is often restricted to trusted managers and secured through access control mechanisms, especially in SNMPv3 environments where sensitive configurations must be protected against unauthorized changes. Due to the potential for disruption, many organizations limit the use of Set operations to specific teams or automated systems governed by strict security policies.

The GetNext operation builds upon the capabilities of the Get request by allowing managers to sequentially walk through the MIB tree. Whereas the Get operation targets a specific OID, the GetNext operation retrieves the next object in the lexicographical order of the MIB hierarchy. This is particularly useful when the exact structure or number of instances within a MIB table is unknown. For example, when a manager needs to collect information from all interfaces on a device but does not know in advance how many interfaces exist, it can issue a series of GetNext requests. Each request will return the next available OID, allowing the manager to traverse the table row by row until it reaches the end. This process, often referred to as an SNMP walk, is crucial for gathering complete datasets from MIB tables such as interface statistics, routing tables, or ARP caches. The GetNext operation helps reduce the need for manual intervention and simplifies data collection across dynamic environments where devices may have varying numbers of resources or configuration objects.

The Trap operation represents a departure from the request-response model of the previous commands. Unlike Get, Set, or GetNext, which are initiated by the SNMP manager, traps are unsolicited messages sent by SNMP agents to managers when specific events occur. Traps enable real-time, event-driven management by allowing agents to alert managers immediately without waiting for the next polling cycle. For instance, an agent may send a trap if a network interface goes down, if a hardware failure is detected, or if a threshold, such as CPU usage exceeding 90 percent, is breached. Because traps are asynchronous, they play a critical role in reducing response times to incidents and enabling proactive network management. SNMP traps are often configured to trigger alarms, open incident tickets, or even initiate automated workflows such as traffic rerouting or system reboots.

Traps can vary widely in terms of complexity. Simple traps may only notify the manager that an event occurred, while more detailed traps include relevant OIDs that provide additional context, such as which interface failed or the severity of the detected issue. It is worth noting that traps do not require acknowledgment from the manager, which makes them lightweight but also introduces the possibility of message loss. To address this, SNMPv2 introduced the Inform operation, a variation of the trap that does require acknowledgment from the manager, improving reliability in critical scenarios where guaranteed delivery is necessary.

The interplay between Get, Set, GetNext, and Trap operations is what gives SNMP its versatility and adaptability. In day-to-day operations, managers typically rely on a combination of Get and GetNext requests to perform periodic polling, collecting a baseline of performance and availability data from devices throughout the network. This polling strategy allows administrators to track trends over time, detect anomalies, and forecast potential capacity issues. Set requests are used more selectively, often for configuration changes or to execute corrective actions triggered by performance thresholds or operational policies.

Traps, meanwhile, serve as the reactive counterpart to polling, providing immediate insight into unexpected events. The balance between these two approaches—polling and event-driven notifications—allows network operators to create highly responsive and resilient network management systems that can adapt to the diverse demands of modern IT environments.

The widespread adoption of these SNMP operations has been facilitated by their simplicity and effectiveness. Whether managing a handful of devices in a small business or overseeing thousands of endpoints across a multinational enterprise, administrators depend on these core operations to maintain visibility and control. Even as newer protocols and telemetry solutions emerge to address specialized needs, the Get, Set, GetNext, and Trap operations remain deeply embedded in the daily routines of network professionals worldwide.

Each of these operations contributes to the overarching goal of SNMP: to enable reliable and scalable network management through standardized mechanisms. Their consistent implementation across multiple SNMP versions ensures interoperability between a wide variety of hardware and software platforms, reinforcing SNMP's position as a key technology for monitoring and managing today's complex and ever-expanding digital infrastructures.

SNMP Walk and Bulk Operations

In the landscape of SNMP-based network management, two operations stand out for their ability to efficiently collect large amounts of data from network devices: SNMP Walk and SNMP Bulk operations. These mechanisms go beyond simple Get requests by allowing administrators and network management systems to retrieve sets of related information in a structured and systematic manner. As networks have expanded in size and complexity, the need to gather comprehensive device and network statistics quickly and with minimal overhead has become critical. SNMP Walk and Bulk operations address this need by streamlining the data retrieval process, reducing the number of individual queries required, and optimizing the performance of SNMP monitoring activities.

SNMP Walk is not a distinct SNMP command but rather a process that relies on successive GetNext operations to traverse a device's Management Information Base, or MIB. The purpose of an SNMP Walk is to sequentially collect data from an entire branch of the MIB tree, starting at a specified Object Identifier and continuing until the end of that branch is reached. For example, if a network administrator wants to gather all interface statistics from a router, they would initiate an SNMP Walk starting from the OID corresponding to the interface table, or ifTable, and continue issuing GetNext requests to retrieve every object under that subtree. Each GetNext request fetches the next OID in lexicographical order, ensuring that all available objects within the specified scope are collected.

The utility of SNMP Walk is most evident when working with dynamic datasets, such as tables of network interfaces, routing entries, or ARP caches. In many cases, network administrators do not know the exact number of rows present in a table ahead of time. A simple Get request would be insufficient, as it targets a single known OID. The SNMP Walk process solves this by automatically traversing each row and column in the table, gathering information without requiring prior knowledge of its size or structure. This automated process eliminates the need for manual intervention and provides a complete snapshot of the target device's operational metrics.

While SNMP Walk is highly effective, it can become inefficient when dealing with very large MIB tables. Since each GetNext request must be sent individually and followed by a response from the agent, the process can generate significant network traffic and introduce latency when dealing with thousands of objects. This limitation is especially noticeable in environments where devices have extensive MIB implementations or where SNMP monitoring is conducted over low-bandwidth or high-latency network links.

To address the limitations of the traditional SNMP Walk, SNMPv2 introduced the GetBulk operation, which was designed to retrieve large amounts of data more efficiently. GetBulk reduces the number of protocol exchanges between the SNMP manager and agent by allowing the manager to request multiple pieces of information in a single query. Unlike the GetNext operation, which retrieves one object per request, GetBulk can fetch entire segments of a MIB table in a single transaction. This dramatically reduces overhead, conserves network bandwidth, and speeds up the data collection process.

The GetBulk request includes two key parameters: non-repeaters and max-repetitions. The non-repeaters parameter specifies the number of objects that should be retrieved using GetNext behavior, typically for single-instance variables outside of table structures. The max-repetitions parameter defines how many objects should be retrieved in bulk from repeating structures such as tables. By fine-tuning these parameters, network administrators can optimize the efficiency of the GetBulk operation according to the specific characteristics of the device and the network environment.

For example, when monitoring a switch with hundreds of interfaces, an SNMP manager might use a GetBulk request with a high max-repetitions value to retrieve multiple rows from the interface table in one message. This reduces the number of round trips required between the manager and the agent and lowers the total processing time needed to gather the full dataset. The GetBulk operation is particularly valuable in data centers, service provider networks, and other environments where scale and performance are paramount.

Despite its advantages, GetBulk is not without considerations. Some network devices, particularly older equipment or devices with limited processing power, may struggle to handle excessively large GetBulk requests. Administrators must balance performance with device capabilities by adjusting max-repetitions appropriately. Additionally, it is essential to ensure that network management systems implementing GetBulk have built-in safeguards to prevent overwhelming devices with requests that exceed their capacity to respond in a timely manner.

The synergy between SNMP Walk and GetBulk is a key aspect of modern SNMP management workflows. In many scenarios, SNMP Walk serves as the default method when working with SNMPv1 or SNMPv2c agents that do not support GetBulk, while GetBulk is used with SNMPv2c and SNMPv3 agents to improve efficiency. Many SNMP tools and frameworks automatically detect the SNMP version in use and select the appropriate method, allowing administrators to benefit from optimized data collection without manual intervention.

Both SNMP Walk and GetBulk operations play a crucial role in building comprehensive monitoring solutions. They enable network management systems to gather the detailed, granular data needed to create real-time dashboards, generate reports, trigger alerts, and feed analytics engines that support capacity planning and predictive maintenance. The ability to traverse MIB trees systematically and retrieve data at scale allows organizations to maintain complete visibility into network performance, detect anomalies early, and ensure service continuity across increasingly complex infrastructures.

In today's network environments, which often feature hybrid cloud deployments, virtualization, and an expanding array of IoT devices, the need for efficient and scalable data collection mechanisms has only intensified. SNMP Walk and GetBulk operations continue to provide network operators with the tools needed to manage this complexity. While newer protocols such as streaming telemetry and API-driven monitoring offer alternative approaches, the familiarity, compatibility, and ease of implementation associated with SNMP Walk and GetBulk ensure that these operations remain widely used in traditional and modern network management systems alike.

The importance of SNMP Walk and GetBulk is not solely technical but also operational. Their ability to minimize resource consumption and optimize network bandwidth while maintaining accuracy and completeness makes them indispensable to any organization relying on SNMP as part of its monitoring strategy. Whether applied to enterprise networks, service provider backbones, or mission-critical industrial systems, these operations empower administrators to maintain visibility and control at every layer of the network.

OID: Object Identifiers Explained

At the core of SNMP's functionality lies the concept of the Object Identifier, or OID. OIDs serve as the fundamental building blocks of SNMP communication, providing a structured and universal way to identify and reference pieces of information within the Management Information Base (MIB) of a networked device. Without OIDs, SNMP managers and agents would lack a common vocabulary for exchanging management data, resulting in ambiguity and fragmentation across network monitoring systems. OIDs are the mechanism that allows SNMP managers to accurately pinpoint specific metrics and configuration variables across millions of devices, regardless of vendor, model, or function.

An OID is a globally unique numerical identifier that follows a hierarchical structure. It can be visualized as a path through a tree, with each number representing a node along the way from the root to a specific leaf, where the leaf corresponds to a managed object such as an interface status, system name, or CPU utilization value. The hierarchical structure is not arbitrary but is carefully designed and maintained by international standards bodies and industry organizations to ensure consistency across different technologies and device types.

The structure of an OID begins at a top-level root, administered by the International Organization for Standardization (ISO) and other entities such as the International Telecommunication Union (ITU). From this root, branches extend into different categories, each representing an organizational level or functional classification. For example, one of the most common OID trees starts with the root 1, which represents ISO, followed by 3 for the identified organization, and 6 for the Department of Defense's Internet branch. From there, the tree might extend into 1.2 for management, 1.2.1 for MIB-II, and so forth. This path, written as a series of integers separated by dots, is how OIDs are conventionally displayed, such as 1.3.6.1.2.1.1.5, which refers to the system name object within MIB-II.

Each level within the OID hierarchy has specific significance. The early nodes of the tree describe broad categories such as the organization responsible for the object's definition, while subsequent nodes provide increasingly detailed classifications down to the individual object itself. For example, under the enterprise branch (1.3.6.1.4.1), which is reserved for private companies, vendors such as Cisco, Juniper, or Hewlett Packard are assigned unique identifiers. From there, each vendor creates their own subtree, defining custom OIDs that describe proprietary features and metrics specific to their devices. This structure ensures that a Cisco device's custom objects will never conflict with objects defined by another vendor, preserving interoperability across multi-vendor environments.

The practical function of an OID is to serve as the address of a specific managed object within an SNMP agent's MIB. When an SNMP manager issues a Get or GetNext request, it does so by specifying the target OID. The agent then responds with the value associated with that OID, which might represent anything from a single numerical reading, such as the amount of inbound traffic on an interface, to a complex table row within a MIB structure. The beauty of the OID system is that it allows SNMP managers to be vendor-agnostic; they simply reference the appropriate OID, and the agent on the corresponding device knows exactly where to retrieve the requested information.

OIDs are more than static identifiers; they are a key enabler of SNMP's extensibility. As new technologies emerge and networking equipment evolves, new branches and objects can be added to the existing OID hierarchy. This flexibility allows the SNMP framework to adapt to technological advancements without disrupting backward compatibility. Standard OID definitions continue to be maintained and expanded by organizations such as the Internet Engineering Task Force (IETF), while vendors regularly publish updated MIBs with new OIDs that reflect changes in their hardware or software capabilities.

Understanding OIDs is crucial for network administrators who wish to create custom monitoring solutions or troubleshoot SNMP-based systems. While most SNMP management tools present data in a human-readable format by translating OIDs into object names using MIB files, the underlying SNMP protocol only operates using the numeric OID form. For example, while an SNMP tool might display the label sysUpTimeInstance for the object with OID 1.3.6.1.2.1.1.3.0, it is the numeric identifier that is sent over the network during SNMP transactions. Knowledge of how OIDs are structured and how to navigate the MIB hierarchy allows administrators to develop tailored monitoring solutions, create custom alerting rules, and integrate SNMP data into broader network management frameworks.

OIDs also play a central role in SNMP Traps and Informs. When a device sends a trap to notify the SNMP manager of an event, the trap message contains OIDs that specify the nature of the event and any relevant details. For instance, a trap for a failed interface might include the OID corresponding to the interface index, the interface's operational status, and the time the event occurred. The manager uses these OIDs to interpret the trap message, determine the severity of the event, and decide on an appropriate response, such as generating an alert, triggering an automation workflow, or initiating further data collection.

One of the notable characteristics of OIDs is their hierarchical scalability. The OID system can represent an almost limitless number of objects due to its tree-based design. Each time a vendor or standards body needs to introduce a new feature or metric, they can simply create a new branch or leaf on the tree. This extensibility ensures that SNMP remains a flexible and future-proof solution for network management, capable of accommodating both legacy devices and cutting-edge equipment.

OIDs are also integral to SNMP's support for complex data structures such as tables. In these cases, the OID serves as both a column identifier and an index within the table. For example, in the ifTable, which holds information about network interfaces, each row corresponds to a specific interface, and the columns represent various attributes such as description, type, and operational status. The OID for a particular cell in this table combines the base OID of the table column with an index that specifies the row. This indexing system allows SNMP managers to access granular information about each individual interface or resource on the device.

In modern network environments, where devices from multiple vendors coexist, OIDs offer a consistent method for standardizing management operations. Whether managing a router from Cisco, a firewall from Palo Alto Networks, or a wireless controller from Aruba, administrators can rely on the structured hierarchy of OIDs to ensure compatibility and consistency in how they collect and interpret monitoring data.

Ultimately, OIDs are the keys that unlock the full potential of SNMP-based monitoring. They are the essential mechanism that ties together the SNMP manager, the SNMP agent, and the MIB, enabling precise and scalable data exchange across networks of any size or complexity. Their hierarchical design, extensibility, and universality ensure that SNMP can remain an adaptable and dependable protocol in an ever-changing world of network technologies.

ASN.1 and BER Encoding in SNMP

In the context of SNMP, the exchange of management information between agents and managers must be standardized to ensure interoperability across devices from different manufacturers. This need for a universal method of representing data is addressed by two critical components: ASN.1 and BER. Abstract Syntax Notation One, commonly abbreviated as ASN.1, is a formal language used to describe the data structures that SNMP employs to represent management information. Basic Encoding Rules, or BER, on the other hand, specify how these ASN.1-defined data structures are serialized into a binary format for transmission over the network. Together, ASN.1 and BER form a foundational layer of the SNMP protocol, enabling devices and management systems to communicate clearly and consistently, regardless of differences in hardware, software, or geographic distribution.

ASN.1 is a language-independent standard developed by the International Telecommunication Union and the International Organization for Standardization. It provides a way to define data types and structures in a manner that is platform-agnostic, ensuring that devices and management systems, no matter where or how they are implemented, can interpret the data in the same way. In SNMP, ASN.1 is used to describe the layout and data types of objects within the Management Information Base, or MIB. Every object defined in a MIB, from a simple integer value to a complex table, is specified using ASN.1 syntax.

The power of ASN.1 lies in its ability to define both primitive and constructed types. Primitive types include basic data formats such as INTEGER, OCTET STRING, OBJECT IDENTIFIER, NULL, and BOOLEAN. These types correspond to the simple values commonly encountered in SNMP management, such as system uptime, interface status, or device names. Constructed types, such as SEQUENCE or SEQUENCE OF, allow for more complex structures that can group multiple primitive types into records or tables. For example, the data representing an SNMP trap message may be defined as a SEQUENCE that includes several related fields, each with its own type and purpose. This hierarchical approach to defining data ensures that even intricate device information can be accurately described and transmitted within the SNMP framework.

ASN.1 also supports extensibility, which is vital in the world of SNMP. As new networking technologies emerge and devices evolve, ASN.1 makes it possible to introduce new types and structures without disrupting existing systems. New MIB modules can be defined to include additional objects using ASN.1, while still remaining compatible with existing SNMP infrastructure. This flexibility has helped SNMP remain relevant for decades, as it can easily adapt to the growing and changing needs of modern network environments.

While ASN.1 defines how data is structured conceptually, BER defines how that data is actually encoded for transport. When an SNMP message is sent over the network, it is serialized into a binary format according to the rules set by BER. This ensures that devices from different vendors can both send and receive SNMP messages in a universally recognized format, allowing interoperability even in heterogeneous networks. BER is one of several encoding rules that can be used with ASN.1, but it is the encoding mechanism that SNMP specifically requires.

BER operates by encoding each piece of data as a triplet consisting of a tag, a length, and a value, often abbreviated as TLV. The tag identifies the data type of the object, such as INTEGER or OCTET STRING, as defined by ASN.1. The length specifies the size of the data in bytes, allowing the receiving system to know how many bytes to read for that particular object. Finally, the value is the actual data itself, encoded in binary format. For example, if an SNMP manager sends a Get request to retrieve the system uptime of a device, the response from the SNMP agent will include an INTEGER type tag, a length indicator, and the binary representation of the uptime value in hundredths of a second.

This TLV structure allows SNMP messages to be compact and efficient, which is critical when operating over networks where bandwidth may be limited. BER also supports variable-length encoding for the length field, which allows it to accommodate both small and large data values as needed. In addition, BER encodes nested data structures by applying the TLV format recursively. For instance, a SEQUENCE containing multiple INTEGER values would itself be encoded as a TLV block, within which each individual INTEGER is also encoded as its own TLV triplet.

One of the key advantages of BER is its self-describing nature. Because every data element includes a tag and length, SNMP managers and agents can parse messages without relying on external schemas. Each message includes all the information needed to decode its contents, making SNMP highly resilient in environments where managers may be communicating with a wide variety of devices, each with different sets of MIB objects. This independence from external schema files also enhances SNMP's scalability, as devices can be added or upgraded in the network without necessitating changes to the core SNMP engine.

However, BER is not without its trade-offs. Compared to more modern encoding mechanisms such as Packed Encoding Rules (PER) or Distinguished Encoding Rules (DER), BER is considered less space-efficient due to its general-purpose nature and the inclusion of additional metadata in each TLV structure. Despite this, BER's flexibility and simplicity have made it an ideal choice for SNMP, where ease of implementation and broad compatibility are often prioritized over maximum compression efficiency.

ASN.1 and BER work together seamlessly to ensure that SNMP's management information can be accurately defined, encoded, and transmitted between managers and agents. The MIB definitions written in ASN.1 establish a common structure for representing device data, while BER encoding translates those structures into a binary form that can be reliably sent over the network. Every SNMP message, whether it is a Get request, a Set command, or a Trap notification, is subject to this process, ensuring consistent and dependable data exchange across the SNMP ecosystem.

In operational terms, most network administrators and even many network management tools abstract away the complexity of ASN.1 and BER, focusing instead on the interpreted values displayed through user-friendly dashboards and reports. Yet, behind the scenes, every OID value, every table row, and every trap received by the SNMP manager owes its precise formatting and interoperability to the meticulous processes defined by ASN.1 and encoded by BER. The SNMP protocol's reliability, extensibility, and ubiquity in network management would not be possible without the foundational role played by these two standards.

By standardizing both the structure and encoding of management information, ASN.1 and BER ensure that SNMP remains a robust and universally accepted protocol. Whether monitoring traditional enterprise networks, virtualized data centers, or the increasingly prevalent world of IoT and cloud-based infrastructures, these encoding and notation systems continue to provide the essential framework that powers the SNMP protocol in modern network management.

SNMP Traps and Notifications

SNMP traps and notifications are essential components of proactive network management, allowing devices to inform administrators of significant events as they happen. While many SNMP operations rely on a polling model, where the manager periodically queries agents for updated information, traps introduce an asynchronous communication mechanism. This event-driven approach enables agents to send immediate alerts to managers, often in response to critical or time-sensitive occurrences such as hardware failures, interface outages, threshold violations, or environmental alarms like high temperatures. The ability of traps to notify managers in near real-time makes them indispensable for reducing response times, maintaining high availability, and minimizing service disruptions.

A trap is a type of SNMP message generated by an agent and sent to an SNMP manager to indicate that a predefined event has occurred on the managed device. Unlike Get or Set requests, which originate from the manager, traps are initiated by the agent and do not require a request from the manager beforehand. This unsolicited nature is what gives traps their value, as they enable devices to report conditions and incidents immediately, rather than waiting for the next polling cycle. This is especially critical in large-scale environments where polling intervals may be several minutes apart, and waiting for the next poll could result in unacceptable delays in detecting and responding to problems.

SNMP traps contain several pieces of critical information that help the manager interpret the event. At the core of every trap is a set of variable bindings, which include Object Identifiers (OIDs) and their corresponding values. These OIDs provide context about the nature of the event, the affected components, and any relevant metrics. For example, a trap reporting a link-down event might include the OID for the interface index, the operational status indicating that the link is down, and a timestamp. The manager receives this information and, depending on the configuration, can escalate the issue through alerts, open a ticket in an incident management system, or even trigger automated remediation workflows.

The structure of traps differs slightly depending on the SNMP version in use. In SNMPv1, traps have a fixed format with specific fields such as enterprise OID, agent address, generic trap type, specific trap code, timestamp, and variable bindings. Generic traps cover common event types such as coldStart, warmStart, linkDown, linkUp, and authenticationFailure. Specific traps, on the other hand, are vendor-defined and offer more granular event reporting. This structure, while simple and easy to implement, has limitations in terms of flexibility and extensibility.

SNMPv2 introduced significant enhancements to the trap mechanism by replacing the fixed-format trap of SNMPv1 with a more flexible notification structure. In SNMPv2c and SNMPv3, traps are sent using the SNMPv2-Trap PDU, which resembles a GetResponse message but is initiated by the agent rather than the manager. This change streamlined SNMP message processing and provided better consistency across different SNMP operations. Additionally, SNMPv2 introduced the Inform message, which is similar to a trap but includes a key difference: informs require an acknowledgment from the manager. This acknowledgment helps ensure delivery reliability, which is particularly important in mission-critical environments where missed notifications could result in prolonged outages or severe service degradations.

Inform messages address one of the primary drawbacks of SNMP traps, which is their use of the User Datagram Protocol (UDP) as the underlying transport mechanism. UDP is connectionless and does not guarantee message delivery, meaning traps could potentially be lost in transit due to network congestion, packet drops, or routing issues. By requiring acknowledgment, informs improve reliability, although they also introduce additional overhead and processing time compared to standard traps.

Traps and informs both leverage the same underlying MIB framework, with events often being defined in standard MIB modules or vendor-specific MIBs. For instance, the IF-MIB defines traps for interface events such as linkDown and linkUp, while enterprise MIBs from manufacturers like Cisco, Juniper, or HP define traps specific to their hardware's unique features, such as chassis alarms, power supply failures, or high CPU utilization thresholds. This extensibility ensures that SNMP traps remain highly adaptable to a wide range of network devices and operational contexts.

In practical network management scenarios, traps are configured on SNMP agents by specifying the destination manager's IP address and community string or user credentials, depending on the SNMP version. Some devices allow for multiple trap destinations, ensuring that redundant managers or backup systems receive critical notifications in case the primary manager becomes unreachable. Additionally, trap filtering and threshold configurations can often be fine-tuned on the agent side to prevent excessive or irrelevant notifications, thereby reducing alert fatigue and focusing attention on the most critical events.

From the perspective of the SNMP manager, traps are typically processed by a dedicated trap receiver or trap daemon that listens on UDP port 162. Upon receipt of a trap, the manager decodes the BER-encoded message, extracts the variable bindings, and correlates the information with its existing inventory and monitoring data. This process often integrates with visualization tools, automated alerting systems, and ticketing platforms, ensuring that the appropriate personnel are notified and the issue is escalated according to organizational policies and service-level agreements.

Traps also play an essential role in enabling automation and orchestration workflows within modern network operations centers. For example, a trap indicating a high temperature on a network switch could trigger an automated sequence that adjusts cooling systems, reallocates traffic away from the affected device, or schedules an immediate inspection by on-site technicians. By integrating traps into automated workflows, organizations can reduce mean time to repair (MTTR) and enhance overall operational resilience.

As networks continue to grow in complexity and scale, the relevance of SNMP traps and notifications remains strong, even as newer telemetry and monitoring protocols gain adoption. Many modern network devices support hybrid models where SNMP traps coexist with alternative notification mechanisms such as syslog, RESTful APIs, or streaming telemetry, providing flexibility in how organizations monitor and manage their infrastructure.

Traps, whether SNMPv1, SNMPv2c, or SNMPv3-based, continue to deliver value by offering lightweight, real-time alerts that help network administrators maintain visibility and control. Their role as a proactive component within the broader SNMP ecosystem complements traditional polling strategies, creating a robust monitoring framework that supports timely detection, diagnosis, and resolution of network incidents across diverse and distributed environments.

SNMP Informs and Their Importance

In the broader context of SNMP's event-driven communication model, informs hold a unique position. While many network administrators are familiar with traps as the default mechanism for receiving asynchronous notifications from network devices, informs offer an alternative that addresses one of the long-standing limitations associated with traps: the lack of delivery confirmation. Introduced in SNMPv2 and carried forward into SNMPv3, informs were designed to provide a more reliable method for agents to notify managers of critical events, while maintaining the simplicity and lightweight nature that SNMP is known for.

The main characteristic that distinguishes informs from traps is the built-in acknowledgment mechanism. When an SNMP agent sends a trap to a manager, the agent does so without any expectation of a response. The trap is sent over UDP, and the agent assumes that the message will be received and processed. However, due to UDP's inherent unreliability and the unpredictable nature of network conditions, traps can be lost in transit. This means that vital information about device failures, environmental alarms, or performance anomalies may never reach the network management system, leaving administrators unaware of issues until they surface in subsequent polling or through end-user complaints.

Informs solve this challenge by requiring the SNMP manager to explicitly acknowledge receipt of the message. When an agent sends an inform, it waits for a confirmation response from the manager. If the acknowledgment is not received within a specified timeframe, the agent can retransmit the inform until either the acknowledgment is returned or the maximum retry limit is reached. This mechanism ensures that critical notifications are far less likely to be silently lost, improving the reliability of event reporting and reducing the risk of undetected issues escalating into major outages or performance degradations.

Beyond the acknowledgment feature, informs share much of the same structure and format as traps. Both are built on the SNMPv2-Trap PDU format and contain variable bindings, including Object Identifiers and associated values, that describe the event being reported. For example, an inform might include information about which interface has gone down, the time of the event, and any relevant environmental metrics such as temperature or power supply status. The ability to package detailed information within the inform allows SNMP managers to quickly assess the context and severity of the event and initiate appropriate responses.

The importance of informs becomes even more apparent in mission-critical environments, where the cost of missing an alert can be severe.

In financial institutions, healthcare networks, or service provider infrastructures, delayed or lost notifications could result in service interruptions, regulatory non-compliance, or reputational damage. By leveraging informs, organizations enhance their ability to maintain network availability and performance while improving incident response times. The acknowledgment process offers a layer of assurance that is particularly valuable in distributed and complex network topologies, where devices may be located in remote or less reliable segments of the network.

Informs also provide operational benefits for automation and orchestration workflows. As enterprises increasingly adopt automated network management systems capable of responding to alerts in real time, the reliability of notifications becomes critical. An inform indicating that a key router has lost connectivity can trigger an automated failover process or reconfiguration workflow. The acknowledgment ensures that the triggering system has received the alert before such automation is set into motion. This synchronization between notification and action helps prevent situations where automation might be executed based on incomplete or missed information.

In SNMPv3 environments, the advantages of informs are further enhanced by the security features inherent to the protocol. While SNMPv1 and SNMPv2c rely on community strings and transmit messages in plaintext, SNMPv3 incorporates encryption, authentication, and message integrity through its User-based Security Model (USM). When an inform is sent in an SNMPv3 deployment, it is secured against interception and tampering, ensuring that only authorized managers receive and acknowledge the message. This is essential in environments where management traffic may traverse untrusted networks or where regulatory frameworks demand strict protection of operational data.

The use of informs, however, introduces additional overhead compared to traps. Since each inform requires a two-way exchange between the agent and the manager, it consumes more bandwidth and processing resources. In large-scale environments with thousands of devices generating frequent events, this can place a heavier load on both the agents and the manager. Administrators must carefully weigh the trade-off between reliability and resource consumption when deciding where and how to deploy informs. In many cases, a hybrid approach is used, where traps are employed for less critical notifications and informs are reserved for high-priority events that demand guaranteed delivery.

Another consideration when working with informs is the configuration of retry mechanisms and acknowledgment timeouts. Agents must be configured to retransmit informs based on a well-defined policy, balancing between ensuring delivery and avoiding excessive retransmission traffic in the network. Similarly, the SNMP manager must be equipped to handle informs efficiently, processing acknowledgments promptly and maintaining logs for auditing and troubleshooting purposes. Many enterprise-grade SNMP managers include advanced inform-handling features, such as deduplication, correlation with related events, and automated escalation rules.

Informs also play a role in distributed and hierarchical SNMP architectures, where intermediate management systems may act as proxy agents or collectors. In such setups, edge devices may send informs to regional collectors, which in turn aggregate and forward processed alerts to centralized management systems. This architecture improves scalability and reduces the load on core management servers while maintaining the reliability benefits associated with inform-based notifications.

While SNMP traps are still widely used and continue to provide valuable real-time monitoring capabilities, informs offer a more robust solution for critical event reporting. Their importance grows in environments where service continuity is paramount and where even a single missed notification could have significant consequences. As network infrastructures evolve and organizations increasingly adopt automation, informs provide the reliable backbone needed to trigger actions with confidence that the alert has been successfully received and processed.

Informs represent an evolution in SNMP's capabilities, addressing the limitations of its earlier notification mechanisms while maintaining backward compatibility and operational simplicity. Their acknowledgment-driven model, combined with SNMPv3's security enhancements, makes informs an essential tool for building resilient, responsive, and secure network management systems in today's demanding IT landscapes. Whether used in conjunction with traps or as the primary notification method in sensitive environments, informs enhance SNMP's ability to serve as a reliable and proactive network management protocol.

Extending SNMP with Custom MIBs

The ability to extend SNMP through custom MIBs has been one of the key factors behind the protocol's enduring success and adaptability. While SNMP provides a universal framework for monitoring and managing network devices, the default or standard MIBs, such as MIB-II, only cover a basic set of general-purpose objects. These standard objects are useful for fundamental monitoring tasks, such as tracking system uptime, interface status, or IP routing information. However, modern networks are composed of highly diverse devices and systems, each offering unique features and operational metrics that often go beyond what is defined in standard MIB modules. To address this diversity, SNMP was designed to be extensible through the use of custom MIBs, enabling vendors and organizations to define their own sets of managed objects tailored to specific devices, services, or operational requirements.

A custom MIB is essentially an extension of the global MIB hierarchy. It is structured and defined using the same syntax and rules governed by the Structure of Management Information (SMI), which specifies how objects are named, typed, and encoded. Custom MIBs are typically created by equipment manufacturers or organizations that need to expose specialized information about their devices or applications that cannot be adequately represented by standard MIB objects. For example, a network switch vendor might create a custom MIB to provide detailed statistics on proprietary hardware components such as backplane utilization, power module status, or advanced queue management settings. Similarly, a storage vendor might define a custom MIB to monitor RAID array health, disk failure alerts, or cache hit ratios.

The process of extending SNMP with custom MIBs begins by registering a unique enterprise number under the enterprises branch of the OID tree, which is located at 1.3.6.1.4.1. Each vendor is assigned a distinct OID subtree beneath this branch, ensuring that custom objects defined by one manufacturer do not conflict with those of another. This namespace isolation is critical for maintaining interoperability in multi-vendor environments where equipment from different manufacturers is monitored by the same SNMP manager. Once an enterprise number is secured, vendors can create sub-branches to define MIB modules specific to their products, with each managed object assigned a unique OID within the vendor's subtree.

Custom MIBs typically contain both scalar objects and tabular structures. Scalar objects represent single-instance variables, such as device serial numbers, software versions, or chassis temperature. Tabular objects, on the other hand, are used to organize sets of related data, such as per-port traffic statistics on a switch or per-disk status information on a storage array. By using tables, custom MIBs can efficiently represent complex data models that allow SNMP managers to query large datasets in an organized and systematic manner.

Defining a custom MIB involves writing the module using the ASN.1 notation as specified by the SMI standard. Each object within the MIB is defined with a unique name, its corresponding OID, the data type (such as INTEGER, OCTET STRING, or Gauge32), an access level (read-only, read-write, or not-accessible), and a textual description that explains the purpose of the object. This documentation is crucial for administrators and monitoring tools to interpret the meaning and expected behavior of each managed object. Once written, the MIB file is compiled and distributed alongside the vendor's device firmware or management tools so that SNMP managers can load the definitions and translate OIDs into human-readable labels.

The benefits of custom MIBs extend beyond device-specific monitoring. Organizations can use custom MIBs to integrate application-level metrics into SNMP-based monitoring frameworks. For example, a company running a proprietary financial trading platform might develop a custom MIB that exposes transaction processing rates, application queue depths, or error counts. By doing so, network operators gain visibility not only into the underlying infrastructure but also into the health and performance of critical business applications, all through the familiar and standardized SNMP protocol.

Custom MIBs also enable advanced control capabilities when used in conjunction with the SNMP Set operation. While SNMP is often associated with monitoring tasks, it can also be used to modify device configurations remotely. A vendor might define writable objects in its custom MIB to allow administrators to adjust system parameters such as threshold values, toggle features on or off, or trigger diagnostic tests. This level of programmability can enhance automation workflows by allowing network management systems to take corrective actions in response to specific conditions detected in the environment.

One of the key challenges when working with custom MIBs is ensuring compatibility with SNMP managers. While the protocol itself can process OIDs in their numeric form, most monitoring tools rely on MIB files to present data in a user-friendly format, complete with object names, descriptions, and data types. Administrators must ensure that all relevant custom MIB files are imported into the SNMP manager or monitoring platform so that the manager can correctly interpret and display the custom data. Failure to load the appropriate MIB files may result in SNMP managers presenting raw OIDs without any contextual information, reducing the readability and usability of the collected data.

In addition to improving network visibility and control, custom MIBs play a significant role in enhancing alerting and reporting capabilities. By exposing specialized objects, vendors and organizations can configure their SNMP agents to generate traps or informs based on the state of custom metrics. For example, a custom MIB might include a trap that is triggered when the input power to a device exceeds safe levels or when a storage array's disk fails. These event-driven notifications provide network operators with actionable intelligence specific to their unique operational context, enabling faster incident response and reducing the risk of downtime.

As networks continue to evolve with the adoption of virtualization, cloud computing, and IoT technologies, the flexibility offered by custom MIBs ensures that SNMP remains relevant. Cloud service providers, for instance, may use custom MIBs to monitor virtual network functions or tenant-specific metrics, while industrial IoT deployments might leverage custom MIBs to report on the operational status of sensors, actuators, and control systems. This versatility enables SNMP to serve as a bridge between traditional IT infrastructure and emerging technology landscapes.

Extending SNMP through custom MIBs is not merely a technical enhancement but a strategic capability. It allows organizations to align their network monitoring efforts with their specific business objectives, tailoring SNMP's functionality to meet unique operational requirements. By leveraging custom MIBs, enterprises and service providers can gain deeper insights into their infrastructure, streamline management tasks, and ensure that their SNMP-based monitoring systems remain agile and responsive to the demands of modern network environments.

SNMP and Network Device Support

The versatility and longevity of SNMP stem largely from its widespread support across an extensive range of network devices. From its early beginnings as a protocol designed for monitoring basic network health, SNMP has evolved into a standard management solution embedded in virtually every network-capable device. Routers, switches, firewalls, wireless controllers, access points, servers, printers, storage arrays, and even power distribution units and environmental monitoring sensors frequently come equipped with SNMP agents, ready to interact with SNMP managers out of the box. This universal support has made SNMP indispensable for network operators, who rely on it to provide centralized visibility and control across heterogeneous and geographically dispersed infrastructures.

Routers and switches are among the most common devices managed through SNMP. These devices form the backbone of enterprise and service provider networks, and their operational health is critical to maintaining seamless data flow between users, applications, and services. SNMP provides essential monitoring capabilities for routers and switches, enabling administrators to track interface status, bandwidth utilization, error rates, and hardware health. SNMP agents running on these devices expose MIB objects that report on the operational status of physical and logical interfaces, including link state (up or down), input and output octet counters, and packet drop rates. In many cases, SNMP is also used to monitor routing tables, VLAN configurations, and device-specific metrics such as CPU load or memory consumption. This real-time data enables network teams to detect congestion, troubleshoot failures, and optimize resource allocation to prevent service degradation.

Firewalls and other security appliances also leverage SNMP to provide critical insights into network protection and traffic flow. These devices often expose MIB objects that report on the number of active sessions, rule hit counts, dropped packet statistics, and intrusion detection system alerts. By integrating firewall SNMP data into centralized management consoles, security teams can monitor traffic patterns, identify potential security incidents, and correlate logs and alerts with network anomalies. SNMP's event-driven capabilities are especially useful in these scenarios, as traps can be configured to notify managers immediately of suspicious activity, such as a sudden spike in denied connections or a failed redundancy system in a clustered firewall environment.

Wireless network devices, such as controllers and access points, are also key beneficiaries of SNMP. Wireless networks are inherently dynamic, with fluctuating client counts, variable signal strength, and environmental factors affecting performance. SNMP enables administrators to collect metrics such as the number of connected clients, signal-to-noise ratios, channel utilization, and hardware health for wireless access points. Wireless controllers, which aggregate data from multiple access points, can provide an even broader view of wireless network health, including roaming statistics and authentication failures. This information is vital for optimizing wireless coverage, troubleshooting client connectivity issues, and ensuring that wireless services meet performance and security requirements.

Servers and data center infrastructure components also widely support SNMP. SNMP agents embedded in server operating systems or baseboard management controllers (BMCs) allow administrators to monitor server health at both the operating system and hardware levels. Typical metrics gathered via SNMP from servers include CPU utilization, memory usage, disk space availability, and process statistics. Hardware-level monitoring through SNMP provides even deeper insights, exposing data related to power supply status, fan speeds, temperature sensors, and hardware faults. In highly virtualized data center environments, SNMP is often used in conjunction with hypervisor platforms to monitor the virtual machine layer as well as the underlying physical hardware.

Storage systems, including SAN arrays and NAS devices, utilize SNMP to report on disk health, array performance, cache hit ratios, and capacity utilization. SNMP agents in these systems expose both standard and vendor-specific MIB objects that help administrators track storage efficiency, detect hardware failures such as disk degradation or RAID rebuilds, and monitor throughput across storage networks. For businesses reliant on data-intensive applications or subject to regulatory data retention requirements, SNMP provides the visibility necessary to ensure storage systems are operating within acceptable parameters and are protected from potential failures that could lead to data loss.

SNMP support is not limited to traditional networking and computing devices. Many facilities and operational technology systems have integrated SNMP agents to facilitate centralized management and monitoring. Power distribution units (PDUs), uninterruptible power supplies (UPS), environmental monitoring systems, and industrial control systems often provide SNMP interfaces to report on power consumption, battery health, temperature, humidity, and other environmental conditions. By incorporating these systems into SNMP-based monitoring platforms, organizations can extend their network management capabilities to cover the physical environment in which their IT assets operate. This holistic view helps prevent outages caused by power failures or environmental hazards such as overheating or excessive humidity.

One of the key advantages of SNMP is its vendor-neutral nature. Unlike proprietary management protocols, SNMP offers standardized communication that ensures interoperability across devices from different manufacturers. Whether managing a network composed entirely of a single vendor or one composed of a wide array of devices from multiple vendors, SNMP ensures that critical operational data can be collected, interpreted, and acted upon through a single management platform. This is made possible by the combination of standardized MIB modules, such as MIB-II, and custom MIBs developed by individual vendors to expose proprietary metrics.

The consistent presence of SNMP agents across so many device types also makes it a foundational technology for network automation and orchestration. SNMP data feeds into automation systems to trigger actions such as traffic rerouting, server scaling, or environmental adjustments. For example, if an SNMP agent on a router reports a link failure via a trap, an automation platform can respond by automatically reconfiguring routing tables to bypass the failed link, minimizing downtime. Similarly, SNMP alerts from PDUs or UPS systems can trigger graceful shutdown procedures or power redistribution to protect sensitive equipment during power disruptions.

Despite the emergence of new protocols and APIs such as NETCONF, RESTCONF, and streaming telemetry, SNMP remains deeply embedded in enterprise and service provider environments. Its simplicity, broad device support, and operational reliability continue to make it an essential component of modern network management architectures. While newer technologies may be used for more advanced analytics or real-time telemetry, SNMP remains the common denominator that binds together legacy devices, contemporary systems, and even emerging IoT devices under a single, unified management umbrella.

The universality of SNMP support ensures that organizations can achieve end-to-end visibility across all layers of their infrastructure, from the data center core to the network edge. As IT environments grow increasingly diverse and distributed, SNMP's role in collecting, reporting, and acting on device and network health data remains critical to maintaining service continuity, optimizing performance, and ensuring the resilience of business-critical services.

SNMP in Data Center Management

In the highly dynamic and mission-critical environment of modern data centers, SNMP plays a fundamental role in ensuring operational stability, performance optimization, and proactive fault detection. As the nerve centers of enterprise IT operations, data centers host an array of interconnected systems and infrastructure components, including servers, storage systems, switches, routers, firewalls, power and cooling equipment, and virtualization platforms. The sheer complexity and scale of these facilities necessitate comprehensive monitoring and management capabilities, and SNMP provides a mature, standardized protocol for overseeing every aspect of a data center's physical and virtual infrastructure.

At the heart of SNMP's value in data center management is its ability to provide end-to-end visibility across diverse devices and subsystems from multiple vendors. Data centers are typically heterogeneous environments composed of equipment from a variety of manufacturers, each offering specialized hardware designed to fulfill different roles. SNMP's support for both standard and vendor-specific MIBs enables network operations teams to monitor the health and performance of all devices in the ecosystem through a unified management platform. Whether it is a core switch from Cisco, a storage array from NetApp, or a rack-mounted server from Dell, SNMP agents embedded in these devices expose essential metrics to the data center's SNMP manager, which collects, aggregates, and correlates the information into actionable insights.

SNMP's role in data center network management is particularly significant. Data center switches and routers form the backbone of internal and external connectivity, handling vast volumes of east-west and north-south traffic. SNMP enables operators to monitor interface status, bandwidth usage, error rates, and link-state changes in real time. Traps and informs sent via SNMP provide instant notifications when links go down, when redundancy protocols fail, or when load-balancing configurations require attention. By continuously monitoring the state of critical network paths, SNMP empowers data center administrators to rapidly identify and resolve bottlenecks or outages, helping to maintain the availability and reliability of applications and services hosted within the data center.

SNMP also plays a critical role in server monitoring within the data center. Whether managing physical servers, blade chassis, or hypervisor platforms, SNMP agents provide valuable insights into system health, including CPU and memory usage, disk space availability, power supply status, fan speeds, and thermal conditions. Modern data centers often rely on SNMP to monitor baseboard management controllers (BMCs) such as Dell iDRAC or HP iLO, which expose out-of-band management capabilities. These interfaces, accessible via SNMP, allow administrators to track server hardware health independently of the operating system, enabling proactive maintenance even when a server's OS becomes unresponsive.

The rise of virtualization and cloud computing has expanded SNMP's role in monitoring not only physical assets but also virtualized resources. Hypervisors like VMware ESXi and Microsoft Hyper-V typically support SNMP agents that provide information about virtual machine (VM) counts, resource utilization, and host availability. SNMP allows data center operators to track performance and capacity trends at the hypervisor layer, helping to optimize virtual machine placement, avoid resource contention, and ensure that service-level agreements (SLAs) are met. Virtual switches and distributed networking components within these virtualization platforms also expose SNMP data, giving administrators granular visibility into traffic flows within virtualized environments.

Beyond the servers and network infrastructure, SNMP's applicability extends to critical environmental and power systems within the data center. Power distribution units (PDUs), uninterruptible power supplies (UPSs), precision cooling units, and environmental monitoring systems frequently include SNMP agents that report key metrics such as power load, battery status, temperature, humidity, and airflow. By integrating this environmental data into SNMP-based monitoring platforms, data center operators can detect and address conditions that might jeopardize equipment health or lead to service interruptions. For instance, if a UPS reports a low battery charge or an elevated temperature reading is detected in a particular rack, SNMP traps can trigger automated alerts, allowing operations teams to take corrective actions such as redistributing workloads, adjusting cooling settings, or scheduling immediate hardware inspections.

One of the most significant benefits SNMP brings to data center management is its ability to support automation and orchestration frameworks. In modern facilities that operate at hyperscale levels, manual intervention is neither sustainable nor efficient. SNMP's integration with automation platforms enables intelligent response workflows based on real-time telemetry. For example, when SNMP detects that a network switch has reached a predefined traffic threshold, the automation system can automatically reassign workloads, reroute traffic, or provision additional network resources. Similarly, hardware failures detected via SNMP traps can trigger the dynamic migration of virtual machines to healthy hosts, minimizing downtime and maintaining business continuity.

Another area where SNMP excels is capacity planning and trend analysis. By collecting historical SNMP data on resource utilization—such as CPU load, memory consumption, network throughput, and power usage—data center managers can predict when additional resources will be needed. This long-term visibility into performance trends helps guide infrastructure investments, ensures optimal resource allocation, and prevents service degradation due to resource exhaustion. SNMP data can also be fed into business intelligence and analytics platforms, providing upper management with insights into data center efficiency, operational costs, and potential areas for optimization.

SNMP's role in data center security should not be underestimated. Many security appliances and devices leverage SNMP to report on access control violations, failed login attempts, intrusion detection alerts, and other security-related metrics. Integrating these security events into SNMP-driven dashboards allows security and operations teams to correlate network and system anomalies with potential threats, enhancing situational awareness and accelerating incident response. Additionally, SNMPv3's support for authentication, encryption, and message integrity ensures that monitoring data and notifications are securely transmitted, protecting sensitive management traffic from interception or tampering.

Despite the growing adoption of modern telemetry systems and API-driven management platforms, SNMP continues to provide a critical layer of observability within the data center. Its compatibility with legacy systems, coupled with its support for the latest enterprise-grade infrastructure, makes it a versatile and future-proof solution. Many leading data center management platforms integrate SNMP alongside emerging technologies such as RESTful APIs, gRPC, and streaming telemetry to provide a holistic view of both physical and virtual assets.

SNMP's ability to unify monitoring across servers, network devices, environmental controls, and power systems contributes to its central role in data center operations. By providing a standardized and efficient mechanism for real-time and historical data collection, SNMP empowers data center teams to ensure maximum uptime, enhance service delivery, and optimize the health and performance of the infrastructure that underpins modern business-critical applications. In an era where data center environments must balance the demands of scalability, efficiency, and reliability, SNMP remains a trusted and essential protocol in the ongoing quest for operational excellence.

SNMP and IoT Devices

The rapid expansion of the Internet of Things (IoT) has introduced millions of new devices into enterprise networks, industrial systems, and consumer environments. These devices range from simple environmental sensors and smart meters to complex machinery and industrial control systems. With this explosion of connected devices comes the pressing need for robust, scalable, and standardized methods of monitoring and managing them. SNMP, a protocol long associated with traditional IT infrastructure, has found a critical role in IoT ecosystems due to its lightweight nature, wide support, and ability to operate in resource-constrained environments. While IoT networks introduce unique challenges compared to conventional enterprise networks, SNMP has adapted to play a crucial role in managing the growing landscape of distributed IoT devices.

IoT devices are typically characterized by limited processing power, constrained memory, and low bandwidth communication links. Many are deployed in remote locations, harsh industrial environments, or embedded within other systems. SNMP's simplicity and efficiency make it particularly well-suited for these constraints. SNMP agents consume minimal resources and operate over UDP, which is lighter than TCP-based protocols and better suited for devices with restricted connectivity or intermittent network access. By embedding SNMP agents into IoT devices, manufacturers enable centralized monitoring and control, allowing operators to oversee vast fleets of devices from a single management platform.

The types of data collected from IoT devices through SNMP vary widely depending on the device's purpose and deployment environment. In industrial settings, SNMP is commonly used to monitor operational technology (OT) systems such as programmable logic controllers (PLCs), remote terminal units (RTUs), and industrial sensors. These devices generate telemetry related to temperature, humidity, vibration levels, energy consumption, flow rates, and other physical conditions. SNMP allows this data to be continuously reported to centralized management systems, where it is analyzed for trends, used for predictive maintenance, and acted upon in real time to adjust control processes. For example, an SNMP-enabled temperature sensor installed in a data center or a manufacturing facility can alert administrators via traps when environmental thresholds are breached, triggering automated cooling systems or maintenance inspections.

In urban environments, SNMP-enabled IoT devices are found in smart city initiatives, where traffic lights, surveillance cameras, streetlights, and environmental monitoring stations transmit real-time status and performance data. SNMP's ability to provide both polling-based and event-driven monitoring makes it ideal for supporting the varied needs of such applications. Periodic polling via SNMP Get and GetNext requests allows city operators to monitor energy consumption and system health across hundreds or thousands of devices. Meanwhile, SNMP traps and informs can provide instant notification of anomalies such as a failed traffic signal, a malfunctioning sensor, or a sudden environmental hazard like poor air quality.

One of the unique challenges in IoT environments is the diversity of devices and protocols. IoT ecosystems often include devices with vastly different capabilities and communication standards, such as MQTT, CoAP, or proprietary industrial protocols. However, SNMP remains an important common denominator, particularly when organizations wish to integrate IoT device monitoring into existing network management platforms. Many enterprise IT teams already rely on SNMP to manage their data centers, campus networks, and remote branch offices, and extending this familiar protocol to cover IoT devices reduces complexity and promotes operational consistency. In scenarios where IoT devices utilize other communication protocols internally, SNMP gateways can serve as translation points, converting native IoT telemetry into SNMP messages that are understood by enterprise network management systems.

SNMP's role in IoT environments is further strengthened by its support for custom MIBs. IoT solution providers frequently develop proprietary MIB modules to expose device-specific metrics and controls via SNMP. This flexibility allows operators to tailor monitoring to the unique characteristics of their IoT deployments. For instance, a smart building system might leverage a custom MIB to monitor occupancy sensors, HVAC controllers, and lighting systems, enabling facilities managers to optimize energy efficiency and reduce operational costs. Similarly, in logistics and supply chain applications, IoT devices such as GPS trackers and RFID readers might expose location data, asset status, and environmental conditions through custom MIB objects, facilitating end-to-end visibility over distributed assets.

Another advantage of SNMP in the IoT space is its compatibility with automation and orchestration frameworks. SNMP data collected from IoT devices can be integrated into larger automation systems that manage workflows across the enterprise. For example, an SNMP trap indicating a high vibration reading on an industrial pump could trigger an automated work order in a computerized maintenance management system (CMMS), dispatching a technician to inspect the equipment before a failure occurs. By combining SNMP telemetry with automation logic, organizations can achieve significant improvements in operational efficiency, safety, and system uptime.

SNMPv3's security enhancements, including authentication and encryption, are particularly important in IoT deployments where devices may operate outside the safety of traditional enterprise network perimeters. IoT devices are frequently deployed in environments where physical access is difficult to control or where network traffic traverses public or semi-public communication infrastructure. SNMPv3 mitigates risks by securing management traffic, preventing unauthorized access to sensitive telemetry, and ensuring that device-generated alerts are trusted and protected against tampering. This is especially critical for IoT systems that control physical infrastructure such as utilities, public safety systems, or manufacturing lines, where a compromised device could result in real-world consequences.

Despite its advantages, the use of SNMP in IoT environments does come with considerations. The lightweight nature of SNMP makes it suitable for many constrained devices, but some extremely limited IoT endpoints may not have the resources to run full SNMP agents. In such cases, lightweight management protocols like CoAP or MQTT may be used on the device side, with SNMP functioning at the aggregation or gateway layer. Hybrid approaches, where SNMP coexists alongside other protocols, are common in large-scale IoT systems. Additionally, SNMP's reliance on polling mechanisms can lead to increased network chatter if not properly configured, especially in deployments with thousands of devices. To address this, many IoT operators fine-tune polling intervals, leverage SNMP traps, and implement event-driven architectures to reduce unnecessary traffic and optimize network performance.

As IoT continues to proliferate across industries such as manufacturing, transportation, utilities, healthcare, and agriculture, SNMP remains a critical tool for enabling centralized management and monitoring. Its ability to bridge the gap between legacy IT environments and emerging IoT ecosystems makes it a valuable asset for organizations seeking to integrate diverse devices under a common operational framework. SNMP's resilience, simplicity, and extensibility ensure that it will continue to play a key role in supporting the reliability, efficiency, and security of IoT deployments as the technology landscape evolves.

SNMP and Cloud-based Infrastructures

As organizations continue to transition to hybrid and fully cloud-based infrastructures, the need for effective monitoring across physical, virtual, and cloud-native resources has become increasingly vital.

Cloud computing introduces a new layer of complexity, as traditional on-premises data centers are now extended by, or even fully replaced with, cloud services hosted by providers such as Amazon Web Services (AWS), Microsoft Azure, Google Cloud Platform (GCP), and others. In this evolving environment, SNMP remains an important tool for bridging the visibility gap between legacy infrastructure and cloud-based components. While cloud-native tools and APIs are increasingly used for monitoring within the cloud, SNMP still plays a key role in hybrid scenarios where organizations must monitor both traditional hardware and cloud-based virtual devices within a single operational framework.

One of the primary use cases for SNMP in cloud-based infrastructures is in hybrid environments where cloud resources coexist with on-premises systems. In such deployments, SNMP agents running on-premises devices such as routers, switches, servers, and power equipment continue to provide critical operational data to centralized SNMP managers or network monitoring platforms. Simultaneously, cloud-based workloads and virtual infrastructure components such as cloud-hosted virtual machines, virtual networks, and storage services must also be monitored to ensure end-to-end service availability and performance. Many organizations solve this challenge by deploying SNMP-capable virtual appliances or network devices within their cloud environments. For instance, virtual routers, load balancers, and firewalls provided by vendors like Cisco, Palo Alto Networks, and Fortinet often include SNMP agents as part of their feature sets, enabling the collection of metrics through familiar SNMP queries.

In cloud-centric networks, SNMP enables monitoring of critical virtual network infrastructure such as virtual private clouds (VPCs), cloud routers, VPN gateways, and virtual firewalls. These components function similarly to their physical counterparts in traditional networks, managing traffic flows, routing, and access controls within the cloud environment. SNMP agents embedded in these virtual devices expose important metrics related to network interface throughput, error rates, latency statistics, and security event counts. SNMP traps and informs can also be configured to notify cloud network administrators of significant events, such as the failure of a virtual firewall cluster, the loss of a VPN tunnel, or the triggering of security policies.

Another key application of SNMP in cloud environments is for monitoring hybrid interconnects. Many enterprises leverage dedicated links between their on-premises infrastructure and public cloud providers through services like AWS Direct Connect, Azure ExpressRoute, or Google Cloud Interconnect. These connections serve as critical pathways for workloads and data exchange between the private and public cloud environments. SNMP agents deployed on the routers and network devices responsible for these interconnects provide continuous monitoring of link utilization, error rates, jitter, and latency. By using SNMP to track the health and performance of these hybrid connections, organizations can ensure that data flows seamlessly between their internal networks and cloud-hosted applications or services.

Although cloud service providers offer native APIs and management tools such as AWS CloudWatch, Azure Monitor, and Google Cloud Operations Suite, SNMP remains valuable for organizations seeking to integrate cloud infrastructure telemetry into existing SNMP-centric monitoring platforms. Rather than relying solely on provider-specific tools, enterprises often require a unified monitoring dashboard that consolidates metrics from both cloud and on-premises resources. SNMP's standardized framework allows data collected from cloud-hosted virtual appliances and infrastructure to be presented alongside traditional network and data center devices. This unified approach improves situational awareness, simplifies troubleshooting, and enhances capacity planning efforts.

Cloud environments also benefit from SNMP's role in monitoring virtual machines and virtualized network functions (VNFs) deployed within Infrastructure-as-a-Service (IaaS) or Platform-as-a-Service (PaaS) models. Many operating systems and application platforms running in cloud-hosted virtual machines support SNMP agents natively or through additional packages. These agents can be configured to report on system-level metrics such as CPU and memory utilization, disk performance, network interface statistics, and service status. SNMP traps can be used to alert administrators when virtual machines experience resource constraints, such as high memory usage or disk space shortages, allowing timely interventions to prevent service disruptions.

In cloud-native environments, where microservices and containerized applications dominate, SNMP can still play a complementary role. While Kubernetes and container orchestration platforms often rely on telemetry standards such as Prometheus or OpenTelemetry, SNMP is frequently used to monitor the underlying infrastructure that supports these platforms. This includes virtual switches, network gateways, and virtualized storage arrays that may be present within the cloud environment or part of a hybrid infrastructure. SNMP data from these foundational layers is essential for diagnosing networking issues, maintaining traffic visibility, and ensuring that the platforms hosting containerized applications perform reliably.

Security is another area where SNMP contributes to cloud-based infrastructure monitoring. Many virtual security appliances in the cloud, including intrusion detection systems (IDS), web application firewalls (WAFs), and VPN concentrators, expose SNMP MIBs for monitoring purposes. These MIBs include metrics on attack attempts, policy enforcement statistics, and traffic filtering logs. By integrating SNMP data from cloud security devices into centralized security information and event management (SIEM) systems, security operations teams gain a broader view of network threats and can correlate cloud-based security events with on-premises activity.

With SNMPv3, organizations managing cloud workloads gain the advantage of enhanced security, including encrypted communications, user authentication, and message integrity. In cloud environments where data may traverse public or shared networks, SNMPv3 helps protect monitoring data from interception and tampering. This is particularly important in multi-tenant cloud scenarios, where maintaining isolation and confidentiality between tenants is critical. Administrators can implement SNMPv3 to ensure that telemetry and management traffic between cloud-hosted SNMP agents and centralized managers adheres to enterprise security policies.

Despite the rise of more cloud-native monitoring and automation tools, SNMP's ubiquity and simplicity make it an attractive option for organizations looking to extend legacy management practices into the cloud. Many cloud service providers recognize this reality and offer virtual network appliances or monitoring gateways that support SNMP. In some cases, enterprises may even deploy their own SNMP-capable virtual appliances within cloud environments to aggregate data from cloud-based resources and forward it to their existing SNMP managers.

SNMP's adaptability ensures that it continues to play a vital role in managing and monitoring hybrid cloud infrastructures. Its integration with virtual devices, its role in interconnect monitoring, and its compatibility with both legacy and modern management platforms allow enterprises to maintain visibility, enforce policies, and respond to issues across highly distributed and virtualized environments. As cloud adoption accelerates and hybrid models become the norm, SNMP provides the essential connectivity required to maintain continuity between traditional network operations and the new generation of cloud-based IT systems.

SNMP Polling vs. SNMP Traps

In SNMP-based network management, two core mechanisms enable the exchange of information between managers and agents: polling and traps. Both methods serve the same fundamental purpose of providing visibility into the state and performance of network devices and systems, yet they operate in fundamentally different ways. Understanding the distinction between SNMP polling and SNMP traps is critical for designing effective monitoring strategies that balance responsiveness, network efficiency, and resource utilization.

SNMP polling is the proactive method by which an SNMP manager queries devices for specific pieces of information at regular intervals. The manager sends requests, typically using Get, GetNext, or GetBulk operations, and agents respond with the current value of the requested MIB objects. This method is systematic and predictable, enabling administrators to gather comprehensive data on device health, performance metrics, and configuration parameters across an entire network infrastructure. Polling can be configured to occur every few seconds, minutes, or at longer intervals, depending on the criticality of the monitored devices and the type of information being collected.

The primary strength of SNMP polling lies in its thoroughness. Since the manager controls the polling schedule and determines which OIDs to query, it can build a complete and consistent picture of the network's operational status over time. Historical performance trends, capacity planning, and baseline comparisons all rely heavily on the consistent datasets generated through polling. Polling is particularly valuable for monitoring gradual changes in network behavior, such as rising CPU loads, increased memory consumption, or growing bandwidth usage on interfaces. By collecting this data regularly, SNMP managers can trigger alerts when performance thresholds are breached or when anomalies are detected in long-term patterns.

However, SNMP polling has its drawbacks. The most notable challenge is the overhead it places on the network and on monitored devices. Frequent polling of hundreds or thousands of devices can generate a significant volume of SNMP traffic, consuming valuable bandwidth and potentially burdening agents with the task of responding to large numbers of queries. This becomes especially problematic in large-scale or geographically dispersed environments, where high polling frequencies may lead to congestion on slower or more expensive WAN links. Administrators must carefully tune polling intervals to strike a balance between data freshness and network efficiency. Additionally, polling introduces a delay in the detection of transient or sudden events. If an interface fails between two polling cycles, it could be several minutes before the issue is detected by the SNMP manager.

SNMP traps, on the other hand, follow a reactive and event-driven model. Instead of waiting to be queried, SNMP agents send unsolicited messages to managers when specific predefined events occur. Traps are lightweight messages containing variable bindings that provide context about the event, such as the affected device, the nature of the condition, and associated metrics. For example, a trap might be triggered when a link goes down, when a device experiences a hardware fault, or when a temperature sensor reports overheating. The key advantage of traps is their immediacy. Because they are sent in real-time as events unfold, traps enable administrators to react swiftly to critical incidents, minimizing downtime and service disruptions.

Traps are particularly effective in environments where certain conditions require urgent attention. By receiving instantaneous notifications of failures or anomalies, network operations centers (NOCs) can quickly initiate remediation workflows, dispatch technicians, or reroute traffic to maintain service continuity. Traps are also more network-efficient than polling, as they only generate traffic when specific events occur, rather than continuously querying devices for information. This makes them well-suited for resource-constrained environments, such as IoT networks or remote field installations, where bandwidth and device processing capacity are limited.

However, traps also come with limitations. Since they are typically sent over UDP, a connectionless protocol, there is no inherent guarantee of delivery. Traps may be lost due to network congestion, packet loss, or configuration errors such as incorrect trap destinations or firewall policies blocking SNMP traffic. To address this issue, SNMPv2 and SNMPv3 introduced the Inform message, a variation of the trap that includes an acknowledgment mechanism to confirm successful receipt by the manager. While informs improve reliability, they also introduce additional overhead compared to traditional traps.

Another limitation of traps is their dependency on agents being properly configured to detect and report relevant events. Not all network anomalies generate traps by default. Devices must be set up to send traps for specific events, and administrators need to ensure that the correct trap receivers are defined in the agents' configurations. Incomplete or poorly maintained trap configurations can lead to critical events going unreported, creating blind spots in network visibility.

In practice, most network management strategies combine both polling and traps to maximize the strengths of each approach. Polling provides the ongoing, consistent visibility required for capacity planning, performance trend analysis, and comprehensive network health reporting. Traps complement this by delivering immediate notifications for urgent conditions that require prompt attention. For example, a network monitoring system may poll switches and routers every five minutes for interface utilization statistics while simultaneously listening for traps that signal link failures, device reboots, or security violations.

Integrating both polling and traps enables organizations to build a monitoring framework that is both proactive and reactive. Polling ensures that gradual performance degradation or subtle configuration drift is detected and addressed, while traps ensure that sudden, high-impact events are brought to light in near real-time. Advanced SNMP managers can further enhance this hybrid model by correlating polling data and trap events, helping administrators prioritize alerts, filter noise, and identify root causes more quickly.

Ultimately, the choice between relying more heavily on polling or traps depends on the organization's specific operational requirements, network architecture, and tolerance for risk. Highly critical networks, such as those supporting financial institutions or healthcare systems, may emphasize traps to minimize the risk of undetected outages, while also maintaining frequent polling for performance monitoring. Conversely, less critical environments or those with bandwidth constraints may opt for lower-frequency polling, relying more on traps to report exceptions.

By understanding the strengths and limitations of both SNMP polling and traps, network administrators can design monitoring strategies that align with their infrastructure needs and business priorities. Combining both approaches ensures comprehensive visibility and timely incident response, supporting the overall reliability, security, and performance of modern networked systems.

Performance Monitoring with SNMP

Performance monitoring with SNMP has become a foundational practice in modern network and infrastructure management. SNMP, as a protocol, was designed to facilitate not just the simple retrieval of device status but also the ongoing collection of performance metrics that provide deep insight into how network devices and systems are functioning under varying workloads. Whether monitoring routers, switches, servers, storage arrays, or other networked devices, SNMP offers a standardized and scalable approach to gathering the data necessary to assess the health and performance of IT environments.

At its core, performance monitoring with SNMP involves the regular querying of device agents for key operational statistics, which are exposed through their Management Information Base (MIB). These metrics can include CPU usage, memory utilization, network interface throughput, packet error rates, system uptime, disk usage, environmental conditions, and many other parameters depending on the device type and the MIBs implemented. SNMP's lightweight nature, based on the UDP transport layer, allows it to collect these statistics efficiently with minimal overhead, making it well-suited for continuous performance monitoring even in large-scale environments with thousands of devices.

Network interface monitoring is one of the most common and essential use cases for SNMP performance monitoring. By querying standard MIB objects such as those found in MIB-II, administrators can gather data on incoming and outgoing traffic volumes, measured in octets, packets, or bits per second. This enables teams to track bandwidth usage trends, detect congestion points, and forecast capacity requirements. SNMP also provides counters for dropped packets, input and output errors, and collisions, which help diagnose network quality issues and determine whether link-layer problems are affecting application performance.

Beyond interface metrics, SNMP allows for comprehensive CPU and memory monitoring on network devices and servers. SNMP agents expose CPU load percentages, available memory, buffer utilization, and memory fragmentation statistics, which are critical for identifying performance bottlenecks and optimizing system resource usage. For example, persistent high CPU utilization on a core router might indicate a need for load balancing or hardware upgrades, while memory shortages on a firewall could point to excessive session table growth or misconfigured policies.

Disk usage and storage system monitoring are also important elements of SNMP performance monitoring. Devices such as servers, NAS devices, and SAN arrays expose SNMP objects related to disk capacity, read and write throughput, IOPS (input/output operations per second), and error rates. By regularly polling these metrics, administrators can ensure that storage systems are not reaching critical thresholds that might lead to service degradation or data unavailability. Moreover, tracking storage performance over time can help with capacity planning, allowing organizations to forecast storage needs and avoid the risks associated with resource exhaustion.

Environmental monitoring is another key aspect of SNMP's performance monitoring capabilities. Many data center devices and network appliances are equipped with sensors that measure temperature, humidity, power usage, and fan speeds. SNMP provides access to this telemetry, enabling operators to maintain optimal environmental conditions for their hardware. Abnormal temperature spikes, power supply failures, or unexpected fluctuations in humidity can be detected and addressed before they escalate into hardware damage or service outages.

One of the main advantages of SNMP-based performance monitoring is its ability to consolidate diverse device data into centralized network management systems (NMS). By leveraging SNMP managers capable of querying agents across a wide range of device types, organizations can create unified monitoring dashboards that provide real-time and historical views of infrastructure health and performance. These dashboards allow administrators to visualize trends, detect anomalies, and correlate metrics from different layers of the network and systems stack. For example, high latency detected at the application layer can be traced back to increased CPU usage on a network device, degraded link performance, or an overloaded storage array.

Trends and baselines play a crucial role in performance monitoring with SNMP. By collecting historical data on key performance indicators (KPIs) over days, weeks, or months, organizations can establish benchmarks for what constitutes normal behavior under different operational conditions. These baselines enable the proactive detection of deviations and gradual degradations that might not be immediately noticeable through real-time monitoring alone. For instance, a steady increase in memory utilization on a critical switch could signal a memory leak or an undetected misconfiguration that, if left unchecked, could eventually lead to service disruption.

SNMP also supports threshold-based alerting, a critical function for performance monitoring. Administrators can configure SNMP managers to trigger alarms when certain metrics exceed predefined limits. When these thresholds are breached, alerts can be sent via email, SMS, or integrated ticketing systems to ensure that the right personnel are notified promptly. For example, an alert may be configured to trigger when bandwidth usage on a WAN link exceeds 80 percent of capacity, or when CPU load on a core firewall remains above 90 percent for an extended period. These proactive notifications enable administrators to address issues before they negatively impact business-critical services.

Additionally, SNMP traps and informs complement the polling mechanism by enabling devices to push notifications to SNMP managers when significant performance-related events occur. Devices can be configured to automatically send traps when certain thresholds are crossed, such as fan failures, temperature alarms, or severe packet loss conditions. These event-driven alerts provide near-instantaneous awareness of critical incidents, reducing the reliance on periodic polling and helping teams respond more quickly to urgent situations.

In modern IT environments, SNMP-based performance monitoring is often integrated with other data sources and telemetry streams, including syslog, NetFlow, and modern API-driven platforms. This multi-faceted approach ensures that performance insights are comprehensive and provide context that might not be available through SNMP alone. For example, SNMP may report high CPU usage on a router, while syslog messages provide additional details about the specific process responsible for the spike. Combining these datasets allows network and systems administrators to make more informed decisions.

Despite the introduction of alternative monitoring protocols, SNMP remains a critical component of performance monitoring strategies in both legacy and modern infrastructures. Its wide adoption, extensive device support, and simplicity make it a go-to protocol for network operations teams. Whether supporting traditional enterprise networks, highly virtualized environments, or cloud-connected infrastructures, SNMP's performance monitoring capabilities remain key to maintaining the reliability, efficiency, and resilience of IT services. By providing ongoing visibility into how devices are operating, SNMP helps ensure that networks and systems perform optimally under both normal and peak loads, supporting business continuity and enhancing the user experience.

Fault Management with SNMP

Fault management is one of the core responsibilities of network and systems administrators, and SNMP has long been a central tool in this discipline. The ability to quickly detect, isolate, and resolve network faults is critical to maintaining the availability and reliability of IT services. SNMP provides a standardized and widely supported protocol that allows administrators to monitor devices for faults in real time and react promptly to network disruptions and system failures. Through its combination of polling mechanisms and event-driven alerts such as traps and informs, SNMP enables organizations to implement fault management processes that are both proactive and reactive.

In SNMP-driven fault management, the manager-agent model plays a key role. SNMP agents embedded in network devices such as routers, switches, servers, and security appliances continuously monitor the internal health and operational status of these devices. These agents expose relevant diagnostic and fault-related information through the Management Information Base, including interface status, system uptime, error counters, and hardware component health. SNMP managers, acting as centralized control points, query this information at regular intervals or receive real-time notifications from agents to identify anomalies or outright failures.

One of the fundamental ways SNMP supports fault management is through interface monitoring. Network interfaces represent critical pathways for data transmission across enterprise networks and the broader internet. SNMP managers can use polling to collect status information from interface MIB objects, such as ifOperStatus and ifAdminStatus, which indicate whether an interface is up or down from an operational and administrative perspective. When an interface unexpectedly transitions to a down state, this typically signals a physical link failure, misconfiguration, or hardware issue that requires immediate attention. Additionally, error counters, such as input and output errors, CRC errors, or packet discards, provide early warnings of degraded performance that could escalate into full outages if not addressed.

SNMP traps enhance fault management by delivering immediate alerts when predefined fault conditions occur. Devices can be configured to automatically send traps to the SNMP manager when critical events take place, such as link failures, hardware malfunctions, power supply issues, or system reboots. These traps contain variable bindings that specify the nature of the fault, its location, and supporting details to help administrators diagnose the issue quickly. For example, a trap generated when a switch port fails will include the OID for the affected port, the timestamp of the event, and other related interface metrics. This real-time fault reporting is invaluable for network operations centers (NOCs) tasked with maintaining 24/7 availability of business-critical services.

In environments where reliability is paramount, SNMP informs add an additional layer of assurance to fault management by requiring acknowledgment from the SNMP manager. This two-way communication ensures that fault alerts are not only sent but also successfully received and logged by the management system. This is particularly beneficial in highly distributed networks or environments where traps may be lost due to network congestion or packet loss. Informs help close the gap between fault detection and incident response by reducing the likelihood of missed alerts.

SNMP's role in fault isolation is also significant. Once a fault is detected, administrators must quickly pinpoint its root cause to prevent service disruptions from spreading or recurring. SNMP provides access to a wide array of metrics and diagnostic data that assist in this process. For instance, in the case of a network slowdown, SNMP managers can query multiple devices to examine interface utilization, CPU load, memory usage, and hardware sensor data, identifying which device or segment is the source of the problem. Furthermore, SNMP can provide visibility into Layer 2 and Layer 3 topologies by exposing data from MIB objects such as Bridge MIB and IP routing tables, helping administrators map the fault's impact across the network.

SNMP-driven fault management is not limited to networking hardware. Servers, storage systems, power distribution units, and environmental sensors all use SNMP to report fault conditions. Servers can alert administrators to power supply failures, temperature sensor alarms, and system crashes. Storage systems can report on disk failures, RAID array rebuild events, or read/write errors. PDUs and UPS systems might signal low battery capacity, overvoltage conditions, or load imbalances. The ability to consolidate these varied fault notifications into a single SNMP management console streamlines troubleshooting and shortens resolution times.

Automation further enhances fault management with SNMP. Modern network management systems are often integrated with automation frameworks that execute predefined workflows when SNMP alerts are received. For example, if an SNMP trap indicates that a critical firewall has gone offline, the automation system might reroute traffic through a redundant path, update network configurations, and notify the incident response team. This integration reduces mean time to repair (MTTR) and mitigates the impact of faults on end users and business operations.

Historical SNMP data also plays a role in fault prevention. By analyzing trends in error counters, hardware health indicators, and environmental metrics, administrators can predict and prevent faults before they occur. For example, a steadily rising temperature reading from SNMP-enabled sensors within a data center might suggest a failing cooling unit. Similarly, increasing interface error rates on a switch could point to degrading cabling or transceivers. By acting on these insights before they escalate into faults, organizations can improve network reliability and avoid costly downtime.

Effective fault management with SNMP also depends on properly tuning alert thresholds and filtering rules. Not every fault condition requires immediate escalation, and flooding operations teams with low-priority traps can create alert fatigue, causing critical events to be overlooked. Administrators must carefully configure SNMP agents and managers to differentiate between routine warnings and high-severity incidents. For instance, traps for minor packet drops might be logged for review, while link-down traps on core network devices might trigger immediate alerts and automated response actions.

SNMP fault management remains a cornerstone of network operations even as modern infrastructures evolve to include cloud, hybrid, and edge computing environments. While newer protocols and telemetry models offer alternative approaches to monitoring and diagnostics, SNMP's widespread adoption, ease of integration, and compatibility with legacy and modern devices ensure its ongoing relevance. From small enterprise networks to massive carrier-grade infrastructures, SNMP provides the essential tools required to detect, diagnose, and respond to faults efficiently, supporting business continuity and the delivery of reliable IT services.

SNMP in Capacity Planning

Capacity planning is a critical process in IT and network management, ensuring that infrastructure resources are adequate to meet current and future demands. SNMP plays a vital role in this discipline by providing real-time and historical data about the performance and utilization of network devices, servers, storage systems, and other critical components. The insights gathered through SNMP allow administrators to make informed decisions about resource allocation, infrastructure expansion, and the optimization of existing assets, all of which are key to maintaining efficient and cost-effective operations.

At the heart of SNMP's utility in capacity planning is its ability to continuously collect performance data from a wide variety of devices. SNMP agents embedded within routers, switches, servers, firewalls, and storage arrays expose a wealth of metrics through their MIBs, including CPU usage, memory consumption, interface throughput, disk space utilization, and many others. By polling these agents at regular intervals, SNMP managers build comprehensive datasets that reflect how devices are performing over time. This longitudinal data is indispensable for identifying trends, forecasting resource needs, and avoiding capacity shortfalls that could impact business services.

Network bandwidth is one of the most commonly monitored aspects of capacity planning with SNMP. By querying interface-related MIB objects, such as ifInOctets and ifOutOctets, administrators can track how much data is flowing through critical network links. These metrics help determine whether network segments are operating within safe thresholds or if they are approaching saturation points that could cause congestion and packet loss. For example, consistently high bandwidth utilization on a WAN link or a data center uplink might signal the need for a bandwidth upgrade or the implementation of traffic optimization strategies. The ability to monitor these usage patterns over days, weeks, and months enables organizations to plan for upgrades in a timely and cost-effective manner, avoiding last-minute responses to unexpected bottlenecks.

CPU and memory utilization are equally important components of capacity planning. SNMP provides visibility into processor load percentages and available memory on devices such as routers, firewalls, servers, and load balancers. High and sustained CPU usage on network devices can indicate the need for hardware upgrades, reallocation of workloads, or the tuning of configurations to improve efficiency. In virtualized environments, SNMP can track the resource consumption of hypervisors and virtual machines, helping administrators determine whether additional physical servers are required or if virtual machine density needs adjustment to optimize performance.

Disk and storage utilization metrics gathered via SNMP also feed directly into capacity planning efforts. SNMP agents on file servers, SAN arrays, and NAS devices expose disk space usage, read/write throughput, and error rates. By analyzing these metrics, organizations can ensure that storage resources are sufficient to meet current application demands while predicting when additional storage capacity will be required. Storage-related SNMP data can also inform decisions about implementing tiered storage, archiving policies, or cloud storage integration to balance performance with cost.

A significant advantage of SNMP for capacity planning is its compatibility with a wide variety of network management systems and analytics tools. SNMP data collected from distributed infrastructure can be fed into performance monitoring platforms that aggregate, visualize, and analyze trends. Dashboards built using SNMP metrics provide at-a-glance views of key performance indicators, while historical reporting functions allow administrators to drill down into specific time periods to assess usage spikes, gradual increases in demand, or seasonal fluctuations. This visibility enables IT teams to plan infrastructure investments based on actual utilization trends rather than assumptions or rough estimates.

Beyond hardware resource monitoring, SNMP supports capacity planning for environmental and power systems within data centers. SNMP-enabled power distribution units (PDUs) and uninterruptible power supplies (UPS) provide data on power consumption, load balancing, battery health, and temperature. These metrics help facilities managers plan power and cooling requirements as data center density grows. For instance, if SNMP monitoring reveals that power draw in certain racks consistently approaches maximum capacity, additional power circuits or cooling systems may need to be installed to support future hardware deployments.

SNMP's role in capacity planning also extends to supporting application and service availability. By correlating SNMP performance data with application-level monitoring tools, administrators can understand how infrastructure resource usage impacts application responsiveness and reliability. For example, network throughput data gathered via SNMP can be linked to application transaction times to determine whether network congestion is contributing to user experience degradation. This integrated approach helps IT teams identify the true root causes of performance issues and prioritize capacity upgrades where they will have the most significant impact.

Forecasting is a key benefit of capacity planning, and SNMP provides the raw data needed to support accurate forecasts. By applying trend analysis and predictive modeling techniques to SNMP-collected metrics, organizations can project when resource utilization will reach critical thresholds. These forecasts inform budgeting and procurement cycles, ensuring that infrastructure upgrades are planned and executed well before capacity constraints threaten business continuity. In highly dynamic environments, such as those leveraging cloud services or virtualized infrastructure, SNMP data helps administrators right-size virtual machine instances, optimize cloud resource consumption, and fine-tune hybrid workloads for cost-efficiency and performance.

SNMP's contribution to capacity planning is not limited to large enterprises or service providers. Small and medium-sized businesses also benefit from SNMP-based insights, enabling them to scale infrastructure incrementally and avoid over-provisioning. In addition, managed service providers (MSPs) use SNMP extensively to track the capacity and performance of client environments, ensuring that service-level agreements (SLAs) are met while proactively advising clients on future infrastructure needs.

Capacity planning with SNMP also supports green IT initiatives by identifying underutilized resources and enabling organizations to reduce power consumption and operational costs. For example, if SNMP data reveals that certain servers are consistently running at low utilization levels, these workloads could be consolidated onto fewer devices, allowing excess servers to be powered down or repurposed. Similarly, optimizing network traffic patterns based on SNMP insights can reduce the load on energy-intensive network components.

In modern IT environments, where infrastructure is often a mix of physical, virtual, and cloud-based resources, SNMP remains an indispensable tool for capacity planning. Its wide device support, lightweight protocol design, and ability to deliver both real-time and historical performance data make it a practical choice for organizations of all sizes. By providing the actionable intelligence needed to predict and prepare for growth, SNMP empowers IT teams to optimize infrastructure investments, prevent performance bottlenecks, and maintain high service levels across their networks and data centers.

SNMP for SLA Monitoring

Service Level Agreements (SLAs) are contractual commitments between service providers and customers that define performance expectations, uptime guarantees, and other critical service metrics. To meet and enforce these agreements, organizations need accurate, real-time visibility into network and infrastructure performance. SNMP, with its broad device support and efficient data collection capabilities, plays a central role in SLA monitoring. It allows organizations to continuously track key performance indicators (KPIs) such as availability, latency, packet loss, bandwidth utilization, and system health across a wide range of devices and platforms.

At the foundation of SLA monitoring with SNMP is the ability to measure uptime and availability of network infrastructure. SNMP agents embedded in routers, switches, servers, firewalls, and other network devices report system uptime via MIB objects such as sysUpTimeInstance. By collecting and logging this data over time, SNMP managers can calculate the total duration a device has been operational, detect reboot events, and correlate uptime metrics with defined SLA thresholds. For instance, if an SLA specifies 99.99% uptime for a critical router, SNMP-collected uptime data enables administrators to verify compliance by calculating downtime across reporting periods.

Beyond availability, SNMP plays a crucial role in measuring network performance indicators such as bandwidth usage and interface reliability. SNMP agents provide detailed statistics on traffic volumes through interface counters like ifInOctets and ifOutOctets, as well as error and discard rates. These metrics allow service providers and enterprise IT teams to assess whether network segments are delivering the level of performance outlined in SLAs. For example, an SLA might guarantee that a dedicated link will not exceed a certain bandwidth utilization threshold or will maintain an error-free transmission rate. SNMP data provides the evidence needed to validate these commitments and to detect when network congestion or hardware faults threaten service quality.

Latency and packet loss, two key metrics in most SLAs, can also be monitored through SNMP, albeit indirectly. While SNMP itself does not measure latency or packet loss as part of the standard protocol, it is commonly integrated with network performance monitoring tools that use SNMP to collect data from probes or devices that run IP SLA tests or similar synthetic monitoring scripts. For instance, Cisco devices with IP SLA capabilities expose results through SNMP, including round-trip time measurements, jitter, and packet loss percentages. This enables operators to monitor critical paths in the network and ensure that latency-sensitive applications, such as VoIP or real-time financial systems, are performing within agreed service parameters.

SNMP traps are invaluable for SLA monitoring because they provide immediate notification of SLA-impacting events. Devices configured to send traps when thresholds are breached, such as link-down conditions or high error rates, help organizations respond rapidly to emerging issues. By leveraging traps in conjunction with regular SNMP polling, IT teams can reduce mean time to detect (MTTD) and mean time to repair (MTTR), ensuring SLA breaches are addressed before they escalate into prolonged outages or service degradations.

Another critical aspect of SLA monitoring is the ability to generate historical reports that document service quality over time. SNMP's ability to collect long-term performance data makes it a cornerstone for producing reports that detail uptime percentages, network performance metrics, and incident response times. These reports serve not only to prove SLA compliance to customers but also as internal tools for identifying patterns, recurring issues, and areas for improvement. SNMP data collected from diverse devices is consolidated into dashboards and analytics platforms where historical trends can be visualized, providing executives and service managers with actionable insights.

In managed services environments, where providers oversee customer networks, SNMP allows for granular, customer-specific monitoring. By segmenting SNMP data collection by customer or service level, managed service providers (MSPs) can tailor their monitoring and reporting processes to meet unique contractual obligations. This may include differentiated alert thresholds, custom reporting formats, or customer portals that provide real-time SLA metrics powered by SNMP-collected data. This level of customization strengthens customer relationships and reinforces confidence in the provider's ability to deliver on contractual commitments.

SNMP's role in SLA monitoring also extends to data center environments where internal SLAs govern the performance and reliability of infrastructure supporting mission-critical applications. Data center operators use SNMP to track the availability and performance of network switches, power distribution units, cooling systems, and server hardware. Ensuring that all infrastructure components meet uptime and operational efficiency targets is essential for maintaining the reliability of hosted applications and services. In cloud environments, SNMP helps bridge the gap between virtualized resources and physical hardware, ensuring that hybrid and multi-cloud workloads also meet internal service objectives.

Security and compliance play a role in SLA monitoring as well. Many SLAs include stipulations around network security, such as maintaining IDS/IPS functionality or firewall uptime. SNMP monitoring of security appliances allows teams to verify that these devices are continuously operational and that they are not reporting excessive alerts, resource exhaustion, or system faults that could impair their protective functions. By integrating SNMP with security information and event management (SIEM) platforms, organizations can correlate performance data with security events, helping to identify conditions where service quality and security compliance may be at risk.

One of SNMP's key advantages in SLA monitoring is its compatibility with automation tools. Automation platforms can leverage SNMP data to trigger workflows that help preserve SLA compliance. For instance, if SNMP metrics indicate that a core switch is nearing a critical resource utilization threshold, the system can automatically reroute traffic to alternative paths, provision additional capacity, or adjust quality of service (QoS) settings to prioritize SLA-sensitive traffic. This proactive use of SNMP data helps minimize service disruption and improves customer satisfaction by maintaining agreed-upon performance levels even in the face of unexpected demand spikes or hardware issues.

Ultimately, SNMP's simplicity, reliability, and ubiquity across network and infrastructure devices make it an indispensable tool for SLA monitoring. It ensures that organizations can validate the delivery of promised service levels through accurate and timely performance data, detect and respond to deviations as they occur, and maintain transparent communication with stakeholders. By providing the data foundation for SLA reporting and enforcement, SNMP supports not only the operational goals of IT and network teams but also the business objectives tied to customer satisfaction, regulatory compliance, and long-term service quality.

SNMP and Syslog Integration

In modern network management, the integration of SNMP and Syslog provides a comprehensive approach to monitoring, fault detection, and incident response. Both SNMP and Syslog are foundational protocols used to collect critical information from devices across IT infrastructures, yet they serve different purposes and offer complementary benefits when combined. While SNMP excels at structured data collection, status monitoring, and event notification through traps and informs, Syslog is a versatile logging protocol that captures a wide array of system events, messages, and alerts directly from the device's operating system and applications.

The key to understanding SNMP and Syslog integration lies in how each protocol gathers and conveys operational intelligence. SNMP is a polling and event-driven protocol that queries specific MIB objects to retrieve well-defined metrics, such as CPU usage, memory consumption, network interface statistics, and hardware health indicators. SNMP traps and informs also enable devices to proactively notify SNMP managers about specific events, such as a failed link, high temperature alarms, or device reboots. However, SNMP messages are typically concise and are designed to convey structured, numeric data about specific OIDs, making SNMP ideal for dashboards, threshold-based alerting, and performance trending.

In contrast, Syslog provides a broader, unstructured stream of messages that detail system-level events, logs, and textual alerts generated by the device's operating system, applications, and services. Syslog messages include various severity levels, ranging from informational messages and warnings to critical alerts and emergency conditions. These logs often provide contextual and descriptive information about incidents, such as authentication failures, configuration changes, software crashes, or firewall rule matches. Syslog is invaluable for root cause analysis and for understanding the sequence of events leading up to faults or security incidents.

Integrating SNMP and Syslog into a unified monitoring strategy enables organizations to leverage the strengths of both protocols. SNMP provides the structured and quantitative data necessary for performance monitoring and automated fault detection, while Syslog offers detailed qualitative insights that are essential for incident analysis and auditing. For example, an SNMP trap might alert administrators that a router interface has gone down, but the corresponding Syslog messages could reveal that the cause was a misconfigured routing protocol or a sudden surge in CPU utilization affecting the router's ability to process packets.

In practical network management workflows, SNMP and Syslog are frequently processed by different but integrated systems. SNMP data is typically collected by network management platforms (NMS) or monitoring tools that poll devices for metrics and receive traps for critical events. These platforms visualize SNMP data through dashboards, graphs, and performance reports, helping administrators track key performance indicators over time. Syslog messages, on the other hand, are collected by centralized Syslog servers or Security Information and Event Management (SIEM) systems, where they are parsed, indexed, and analyzed for event correlation, forensic investigations, and compliance reporting.

One of the primary advantages of SNMP and Syslog integration is enhanced situational awareness. By correlating SNMP traps and Syslog messages within a unified incident management platform, organizations can gain deeper insights into complex incidents. For instance, if a network switch generates an SNMP trap indicating a fan failure, Syslog logs from the same device may provide additional information about increasing device temperatures, power fluctuations, or other hardware anomalies that preceded the failure. This correlation allows for more accurate incident diagnosis and faster resolution times.

Syslog also complements SNMP by providing visibility into events that may not be exposed via SNMP MIBs. Many application-level events, security logs, and detailed system alerts are only available through Syslog. For example, firewall devices might send SNMP traps for link status changes but rely on Syslog to report on denied connections, intrusion detection alerts, or VPN session logs. Without Syslog integration, critical security and operational details may be missed, limiting the effectiveness of incident response and network troubleshooting.

Another benefit of integrating SNMP and Syslog is the ability to create more precise alerting rules. Advanced monitoring platforms can ingest both SNMP and Syslog data streams and apply correlation logic to reduce false positives and improve the relevance of alerts. For example, receiving an SNMP trap indicating high memory usage on a firewall might not warrant immediate escalation. However, if Syslog data simultaneously reports repeated authentication failures or resource exhaustion warnings from security services running on the same device, the combined insight may trigger a high-priority incident response due to the elevated risk.

The integration also supports regulatory compliance and audit requirements. Many industries require organizations to retain comprehensive logs and monitoring data for security audits, forensic investigations, and incident reporting. Combining SNMP performance data with Syslog event logs provides a complete record of both system metrics and contextual event details. This ensures that organizations can demonstrate full accountability for how infrastructure events were detected, diagnosed, and resolved.

From an architectural standpoint, integrating SNMP and Syslog requires coordinated configuration across devices and monitoring systems. Network devices must be configured to send SNMP traps to SNMP managers and forward Syslog messages to centralized Syslog servers. On the receiving end, monitoring platforms must be capable of processing and correlating these data streams, often through the use of APIs, log parsers, or built-in integrations. Modern SIEM systems and network management platforms increasingly support native SNMP and Syslog integration, providing unified dashboards and incident views that consolidate both types of telemetry.

Automation workflows also benefit from SNMP and Syslog integration. Network automation tools can use SNMP traps as triggers for automated remediation, while Syslog data can provide confirmation that corrective actions have succeeded or identify additional issues that require further attention. For example, if a router generates an SNMP trap indicating a failed link, an automation platform might reroute traffic while simultaneously monitoring Syslog messages from adjacent devices to detect cascading impacts, such as increased load on backup links or protocol re-convergence messages from dynamic routing processes.

Finally, as organizations increasingly adopt hybrid and cloud-native infrastructures, SNMP and Syslog remain relevant and complementary. Virtualized network functions, cloud-based firewalls, and virtual machines often still support both SNMP and Syslog, allowing consistent monitoring across on-premises and cloud environments. This consistency helps organizations maintain visibility and control over highly distributed infrastructures, ensuring that performance and security standards are upheld regardless of where resources are located.

The integration of SNMP and Syslog represents a powerful combination for IT and network operations teams. Together, they provide a more holistic view of infrastructure health, improve incident detection and response, and support long-term operational improvements through actionable insights and comprehensive reporting. By leveraging both protocols in tandem, organizations can significantly enhance their ability to manage complex and ever-evolving IT environments.

SNMP and NetFlow: Complementary Technologies

SNMP and NetFlow are two of the most widely used technologies in the realm of network monitoring and management. While each serves distinct purposes, they are inherently complementary and, when used together, provide a more complete picture of network health, performance, and usage patterns. SNMP is primarily focused on gathering device-level statistics and operational metrics, whereas NetFlow offers granular insights into traffic flows, providing visibility into who is communicating, over which protocols, and how much bandwidth is being consumed by specific conversations. Combining SNMP and NetFlow enables network administrators to diagnose issues more effectively, optimize performance, and enforce security and compliance policies with greater precision.

SNMP, as a protocol, has long been the standard for device-level monitoring. It allows administrators to collect real-time and historical performance data from routers, switches, firewalls, servers, and a broad array of other network devices. SNMP agents expose data through MIB objects, including metrics such as CPU usage, memory consumption, disk space, interface status, and bandwidth utilization. This information is critical for understanding how well network infrastructure components are performing, detecting hardware faults, and identifying bottlenecks at the device level. SNMP polling provides a baseline view of resource utilization and health across an entire network.

However, SNMP's device-centric view does not provide details about the nature of the traffic traversing the network. For example, while SNMP can reveal that an interface is experiencing high bandwidth usage, it does not explain what types of traffic are causing the spike, which hosts are involved, or which applications are responsible. This is where NetFlow becomes essential. NetFlow, originally developed by Cisco, is a protocol that collects detailed flow-level data from network devices. A flow is defined as a unidirectional sequence of packets sharing common attributes such as source and destination IP addresses, source and destination ports, protocol type, and ingress/egress interfaces.

NetFlow data provides the application-layer visibility that SNMP lacks. It reveals not just how much traffic is passing through a device, but who is communicating, the nature of the communication, and how long each session lasts. For instance, NetFlow can indicate that a sudden increase in traffic on a router's WAN interface is caused by large file transfers from a specific server to multiple remote clients, or that an unusual spike in UDP traffic is associated with a potential denial-of-service attack. This level of insight is critical for security, troubleshooting, and network capacity planning.

The integration of SNMP and NetFlow allows organizations to correlate infrastructure health data with detailed traffic analytics. For example, if SNMP monitoring shows high CPU utilization on a router, NetFlow data might reveal that the router is processing a large volume of short-lived TCP sessions, possibly due to application misbehavior or a security incident. Similarly, if SNMP detects that a network link is saturated, NetFlow can identify whether the congestion is due to business-critical applications, recreational usage, or unauthorized data exfiltration attempts. By using both technologies together, network administrators can move beyond simply identifying that a problem exists to understanding its root cause and developing appropriate corrective actions.

SNMP is also highly effective in helping administrators maintain operational baselines. By polling for metrics like interface utilization, device memory usage, and packet error rates, SNMP establishes what normal operating conditions look like across the infrastructure. This enables network operations teams to detect gradual performance degradations, misconfigurations, or device aging before they escalate into service-impacting issues. NetFlow complements this capability by revealing deviations in traffic patterns. For example, an organization might have a baseline showing typical traffic levels during business hours, but NetFlow could highlight anomalies such as unauthorized peer-to-peer traffic or unexpected data transfers to external destinations outside normal working hours.

Another benefit of combining SNMP and NetFlow is in capacity planning and optimization. SNMP data is invaluable for tracking device-level resource utilization and identifying under or overutilized links, switches, or routers. NetFlow data, on the other hand, provides the context behind that utilization by breaking down the specific types of traffic contributing to resource consumption. This combined visibility allows organizations to make more informed decisions about infrastructure investments, such as upgrading circuits, balancing loads more efficiently, or segmenting traffic through quality of service (QoS) policies to prioritize critical applications.

From a security perspective, SNMP and NetFlow work together to strengthen network defenses. SNMP monitors the health of firewalls, intrusion prevention systems, and network infrastructure devices, ensuring they are operating within acceptable thresholds. NetFlow provides real-time intelligence on traffic behavior, allowing security teams to detect reconnaissance activity, unauthorized data transfers, or distributed denial-of-service (DDoS) patterns. While SNMP may raise an alert when a firewall's CPU utilization spikes or when a port goes down, NetFlow will show whether that spike correlates with unusual outbound traffic or malicious scanning attempts originating from within the network.

SNMP and NetFlow are also complementary when it comes to automation and incident response. Automated network management platforms can trigger workflows based on SNMP alerts and enrich them with contextual NetFlow data. For instance, if SNMP reports that a critical uplink is operating at 95% capacity, the system could automatically retrieve NetFlow data to identify the top talkers or top applications contributing to the load. This integration shortens the time required for root cause analysis and supports faster remediation through automated policies, such as rate limiting or redirecting non-essential traffic.

The deployment of SNMP and NetFlow is typically straightforward, given their broad support across network devices. Most enterprise-grade switches and routers come with SNMP agents enabled by default and offer configurable NetFlow or NetFlow-compatible export capabilities, such as IPFIX or sFlow. SNMP managers and NetFlow collectors can be deployed separately or integrated into a single network management solution, providing administrators with a centralized view of both infrastructure health and traffic analytics.

Despite the rise of newer monitoring technologies and telemetry protocols, SNMP and NetFlow remain indispensable due to their maturity, scalability, and widespread adoption. Together, they provide a powerful and holistic approach to network visibility, helping organizations manage increasingly complex infrastructures with greater accuracy and efficiency. By leveraging SNMP for infrastructure monitoring and NetFlow for traffic analysis, organizations can ensure optimal network performance, secure their assets, and make smarter operational decisions that align with business goals.

SNMP and Automation in Network Management

The combination of SNMP and automation has transformed how organizations manage their networks, driving efficiency, consistency, and faster response times. As networks continue to grow in complexity and scale, manual management processes are no longer sufficient to meet the demands of modern IT infrastructures. SNMP, with its standardized and lightweight protocol for monitoring and controlling devices, has become a cornerstone of network automation initiatives. By leveraging SNMP's capabilities alongside automation frameworks, organizations are able to streamline repetitive tasks, accelerate incident response, and improve the overall health and performance of their networks.

At the heart of this integration is SNMP's ability to collect real-time operational data from devices such as routers, switches, servers, firewalls, load balancers, and storage systems. SNMP agents embedded in these devices expose metrics and status indicators via MIBs, providing automation platforms with continuous visibility into network conditions. By automating the retrieval of SNMP data, administrators can eliminate the need for manual polling and monitoring, freeing up valuable time to focus on higher-level strategic initiatives. Automation tools can be configured to regularly gather SNMP metrics such as interface utilization, device uptime, CPU load, memory consumption, and environmental readings from thousands of devices simultaneously.

One of the most powerful applications of SNMP in automation is in proactive fault detection and resolution. SNMP traps and informs enable devices to send unsolicited notifications to automation systems when critical events occur, such as a link failure, hardware malfunction, or security breach. When an automation platform receives these alerts, it can trigger predefined workflows that take immediate corrective action. For example, if an SNMP trap indicates that a switch port has gone down, the automation system might reconfigure routing tables to reroute traffic through redundant links, notify relevant personnel via messaging platforms, and log the incident for future analysis, all without manual intervention.

SNMP also plays a key role in automating routine network maintenance tasks. Automation platforms can use SNMP data to identify when specific maintenance actions are required and execute them accordingly. For instance, if SNMP polling detects that a device's memory utilization has consistently exceeded a set threshold over several polling cycles, the system can automatically schedule a memory-clearing script or reassign traffic loads to other devices to balance resource consumption. This type of closed-loop automation reduces human error, enhances network resiliency, and ensures that minor issues are resolved before they escalate into critical incidents.

Configuration management is another area where SNMP and automation intersect. While SNMP itself is often associated with monitoring and fault management, it also supports control capabilities through the SNMP Set operation. This feature allows automation platforms to remotely adjust device settings, toggle features, or apply configuration changes based on real-time SNMP data. For example, an automation workflow could detect that a specific VLAN is experiencing traffic saturation and automatically reassign certain endpoints to a different VLAN by using SNMP Set commands to update the necessary configuration objects on network switches.

Automation frameworks integrated with SNMP also play a crucial role in incident prioritization and resource optimization. By continuously analyzing SNMP data across the network, automation platforms can identify trends and allocate resources accordingly. If SNMP metrics indicate that certain devices or segments are underutilized while others are consistently overloaded, the automation system can dynamically redistribute traffic or adjust service levels to optimize performance and reduce the risk of outages. This intelligent resource allocation not only improves the user experience but also extends the lifespan of critical infrastructure by avoiding unnecessary strain on network components.

The integration of SNMP with automation systems also enhances the accuracy and effectiveness of root cause analysis. By correlating SNMP data with logs, telemetry, and other network events, automation tools can help identify the true source of problems and initiate corrective actions without requiring manual troubleshooting. For instance, if SNMP metrics show high CPU usage on a router at the same time that interface error counters are increasing, the automation system can deduce that the device is under excessive load and execute mitigation measures such as load balancing or service reallocation.

In addition to fault remediation, SNMP-driven automation is increasingly used for service provisioning and deprovisioning. For example, when onboarding new devices or services, automation platforms can use SNMP to verify network readiness by polling devices for available capacity, link status, and health indicators. Once confirmed, the automation workflow can proceed to configure the necessary network settings, apply access control policies, and provision new services seamlessly. Conversely, when services are retired or decommissioned, automation systems can use SNMP data to ensure that unused interfaces and configurations are cleaned up, preventing configuration drift and reducing security risks.

SNMP and automation also play an important role in supporting compliance and audit requirements. Automated processes can continuously monitor SNMP metrics to ensure that devices meet operational and security policies. If non-compliant conditions are detected, such as outdated firmware versions, unauthorized configuration changes, or resource usage outside of defined thresholds, the automation system can take corrective action and generate reports for auditing purposes. This capability helps organizations adhere to regulatory requirements and internal governance frameworks, reducing the risk of non-compliance penalties.

In hybrid and multi-cloud environments, SNMP-driven automation extends beyond traditional network devices to include virtual appliances, cloud gateways, and edge infrastructure. Virtual network functions (VNFs) and cloud-based firewalls often expose SNMP MIBs, enabling automation platforms to apply the same monitoring and control strategies used on physical infrastructure to virtualized resources. This consistency simplifies operations, supports workload mobility, and helps organizations maintain visibility and control across distributed environments.

The combination of SNMP and automation empowers network operations teams to achieve greater agility, reduce operational costs, and improve service reliability. By automating tasks that were traditionally manual, repetitive, and time-consuming, organizations can ensure faster incident resolution, reduce human errors, and free up resources to focus on innovation and strategic initiatives. The synergy between SNMP's rich telemetry capabilities and automation's ability to translate data into action is essential for modern network management, particularly as organizations face increasing pressure to deliver high-performance, resilient, and scalable IT services.

SNMP for Wireless Network Monitoring

Wireless networks have become a critical component of modern IT infrastructures, supporting a wide range of devices and services in both enterprise and public environments. As organizations rely more heavily on wireless connectivity to enable mobility, flexibility, and productivity, the need for comprehensive wireless network monitoring has grown significantly. SNMP, with its standardized approach to collecting performance and status data from network devices, plays a key role in ensuring the reliability, efficiency, and security of wireless networks. By leveraging SNMP, administrators gain visibility into wireless access points, wireless LAN controllers, and the entire wireless ecosystem to detect issues, optimize performance, and maintain service quality.

Wireless networks present unique challenges compared to wired networks. Signal strength fluctuations, radio frequency interference, client mobility, and bandwidth contention all contribute to the complexity of managing wireless environments. SNMP simplifies this task by providing access to a variety of MIB objects that expose critical information about wireless infrastructure components. Wireless access points and controllers equipped with SNMP agents publish telemetry related to radio frequencies, client associations, channel utilization, error rates, and other key wireless parameters. By regularly polling these agents or receiving SNMP traps, administrators can track wireless performance trends and respond quickly to emerging issues.

One of the most fundamental metrics monitored through SNMP in wireless networks is client association status. Wireless access points report the number of connected clients, along with detailed information such as signal strength (RSSI), noise levels, data rates, and session durations. Monitoring client associations helps administrators identify overloaded access points, coverage gaps, and roaming patterns that could impact user experience. For example, if SNMP data reveals that a particular access point consistently has a higher number of clients than neighboring access points, this may indicate a need for load balancing or additional AP deployment to improve coverage and distribute client load more evenly.

SNMP also enables monitoring of channel utilization and interference, two of the most common causes of degraded wireless network performance. Access points operating in crowded environments often experience co-channel and adjacent-channel interference, which can result in packet loss, reduced throughput, and increased latency. SNMP exposes metrics related to channel occupancy, allowing administrators to identify which channels are heavily utilized and which are underused. This insight supports dynamic channel planning and adjustment strategies, where wireless LAN controllers or automation systems can automatically reassign channels based on real-time SNMP data to minimize interference and optimize spectrum usage.

Another critical aspect of wireless network monitoring with SNMP is tracking signal quality and environmental conditions. SNMP-enabled access points provide data on metrics such as signal-to-noise ratio (SNR), transmission retries, and frame error rates. These indicators help network teams detect physical-layer issues that may be invisible to upper-layer monitoring tools. For instance, a low SNR value detected via SNMP may suggest the presence of physical obstructions, interference from non-Wi-Fi devices, or poor antenna placement. By correlating SNMP-reported signal quality metrics with client performance data, administrators can fine-tune radio configurations, adjust transmit power settings, and recommend physical adjustments to improve wireless performance.

SNMP traps play an important role in proactive wireless network management by enabling devices to send immediate notifications of significant events. Access points and controllers can be configured to generate traps for conditions such as AP failures, rogue AP detection, excessive retransmissions, or unauthorized client associations. These real-time alerts allow administrators to take swift action, minimizing the impact on users and reducing downtime. For example, if an SNMP trap reports the detection of a rogue access point broadcasting within a secured environment, security teams can investigate and mitigate potential threats before they compromise sensitive data.

Wireless LAN controllers (WLCs) enhance the SNMP monitoring process by centralizing the management of multiple access points across large environments. SNMP polling of WLCs provides aggregated views of wireless network health, consolidating data such as total client counts, AP status, firmware versions, and system resource usage. Additionally, WLCs often expose advanced SNMP metrics related to authentication failures, wireless encryption protocols in use, and policy enforcement statistics. This centralized telemetry helps administrators ensure that wireless services are not only performant but also aligned with security and compliance requirements.

SNMP-based wireless network monitoring is also essential for capacity planning. By analyzing long-term SNMP data, organizations can forecast wireless demand growth, identify recurring congestion points, and plan future access point deployments more effectively. For example, trends indicating steadily increasing client counts in specific locations may suggest the need for additional access points to accommodate growth and maintain service quality. Similarly, persistent high utilization of certain frequency bands could drive the decision to deploy dual-band or tri-band APs to spread the load more evenly across available spectrum.

In environments where seamless mobility is critical, such as hospitals, warehouses, and large corporate campuses, SNMP provides insights into client roaming behavior. Access points report data on roaming events, handoff times, and client dwell times, which help identify areas where roaming performance may be suboptimal. Poorly tuned roaming parameters or coverage holes can lead to frequent client disconnections and service interruptions. By continuously monitoring SNMP data related to client transitions, administrators can optimize mobility parameters such as roaming thresholds, transmit power settings, and AP placement to support a smoother roaming experience.

Another benefit of SNMP in wireless network monitoring is its ability to integrate with existing network management systems and automation platforms. SNMP-collected wireless metrics can be incorporated into centralized dashboards that display both wired and wireless network health side by side. This holistic visibility is critical in hybrid environments where both types of infrastructure work together to deliver end-to-end connectivity. By combining SNMP data from access points, switches, routers, and controllers, administrators gain full visibility into how wireless clients interact with the broader network, allowing for more accurate troubleshooting and optimization.

SNMP also supports security monitoring within wireless networks. Many WLCs and APs expose SNMP data related to wireless intrusion detection systems (WIDS), rogue AP detection, and wireless authentication anomalies. This enables security teams to integrate SNMP-collected data into SIEM platforms and incident response workflows, improving the organization's ability to detect and mitigate wireless-specific security threats. For example, SNMP traps reporting frequent authentication failures may indicate a brute-force attack attempt against the wireless network, prompting immediate investigation and countermeasures.

In modern enterprise environments, where wireless connectivity has become the default method of network access for employees, guests, and IoT devices, the role of SNMP in wireless network monitoring has never been more important. Its standardized approach to collecting and reporting wireless performance data, combined with its ability to provide both real-time alerts and historical trend analysis, makes SNMP an indispensable tool for network operations teams. By leveraging SNMP effectively, organizations can ensure that their wireless networks deliver the reliability, performance, and security necessary to support business-critical applications and services.

SNMP and Virtualization Environments

As enterprises continue to adopt virtualization technologies to improve resource utilization, flexibility, and scalability, the need for effective monitoring tools that extend into these virtualized environments becomes paramount. SNMP, traditionally associated with physical network and infrastructure management, has evolved to remain highly relevant within virtualized infrastructures. While virtualization platforms introduce new layers of abstraction, SNMP still plays a crucial role in providing visibility into the health and performance of both virtual and underlying physical resources, enabling administrators to monitor, manage, and optimize complex virtualized environments effectively.

Virtualization environments, such as those built on VMware vSphere, Microsoft Hyper-V, KVM, or Xen, rely on hypervisors to host multiple virtual machines (VMs) on a single physical server. These hypervisors, along with virtual switches, virtual storage controllers, and virtualized network functions, all generate operational data that must be monitored to ensure consistent performance and availability. SNMP agents installed on hypervisors or integrated into management platforms expose critical telemetry related to system resource utilization, VM status, and hypervisor health.

One of the key metrics that SNMP provides within virtualization environments is hypervisor resource usage. Hypervisors allocate CPU, memory, storage, and network resources among all hosted VMs. SNMP enables administrators to monitor CPU utilization at the hypervisor level, giving insight into how effectively resources are being distributed and identifying when contention arises between VMs. Similarly, SNMP agents report on memory consumption, swap activity, and memory ballooning, which are critical indicators of whether the hypervisor is experiencing memory overcommitment. These metrics help administrators detect capacity issues early and take corrective actions, such as migrating VMs to less burdened hosts or provisioning additional hardware resources.

In addition to hypervisor-level monitoring, SNMP provides detailed insights into virtual switch operations. Virtual switches play an essential role in directing traffic between VMs, physical networks, and virtual appliances. SNMP exposes MIB objects that detail interface status, throughput, packet loss, and error rates on virtual switch ports. By monitoring these metrics, administrators can ensure that virtual networking infrastructure is functioning properly and that virtualized traffic is flowing without interruption or degradation. Identifying high interface utilization, packet discards, or errors at the virtual switch layer is essential for troubleshooting communication issues between VMs or between VMs and external networks.

SNMP also supports visibility into the virtual machine layer itself. Many virtualization platforms expose SNMP data regarding the status of individual VMs, including uptime, power state, and resource consumption. Administrators can monitor VM CPU and memory usage trends over time to identify which virtual machines are over-consuming resources or underutilized. This insight enables workload optimization efforts, such as resizing VMs, redistributing workloads across hosts, or consolidating services to free up resources.

Another critical application of SNMP in virtualization environments is in monitoring storage subsystems. Virtualized environments often rely on shared storage architectures, such as SAN or NAS, to host virtual machine disk files (VMDKs or virtual hard disks). SNMP agents on storage arrays expose valuable telemetry such as disk I/O performance, storage capacity usage, latency metrics, and disk health. Monitoring this data helps ensure that storage performance aligns with the demands of the virtual infrastructure and allows administrators to detect storage bottlenecks that may affect VM performance.

SNMP traps and informs are equally valuable in virtualized environments. Hypervisors, virtual switches, and storage systems can be configured to send traps for critical events such as host hardware failures, storage array capacity warnings, or network link down conditions. In highly dynamic virtualized environments, where workloads and configurations change frequently, receiving real-time notifications of these events helps administrators respond quickly and maintain high service availability.

SNMP also integrates well with virtualization management platforms and orchestration tools. Many virtualization solutions, such as VMware vCenter or Microsoft System Center Virtual Machine Manager, include SNMP support, allowing centralized monitoring platforms to collect data directly from these management consoles. This integration provides a holistic view of both the physical and virtual layers of the environment. For example, SNMP monitoring can simultaneously track hardware health metrics on the physical server, such as fan speeds, power supply status, and chassis temperature, alongside hypervisor and VM performance indicators. This end-to-end visibility is critical for troubleshooting issues that may span multiple layers of the stack.

Furthermore, SNMP plays an important role in capacity planning within virtualized environments. Historical SNMP data helps administrators track resource consumption trends over time, enabling more accurate forecasting of when additional compute, storage, or network capacity will be needed. By correlating hypervisor-level metrics with workload patterns, organizations can make informed decisions about when to invest in additional infrastructure or optimize existing resource allocations. For example, consistently high CPU usage on a cluster of hypervisors may suggest the need to deploy additional physical servers or rebalance VMs to prevent performance degradation.

Security monitoring is another area where SNMP adds value in virtualized infrastructures. Virtualized firewalls, intrusion detection systems, and network segmentation policies all generate SNMP telemetry. Security teams can use SNMP data to ensure that these virtual security appliances are functioning correctly, enforcing access control policies, and maintaining secure boundaries between tenants or applications. SNMP traps can alert administrators to security events such as failed login attempts on management interfaces or unusual traffic patterns detected by virtual IDS systems.

In cloud and hybrid environments where virtualization platforms are extended to public cloud services, SNMP can still serve as a bridge between traditional infrastructure and cloud-based resources. Many cloud service providers support SNMP-compatible virtual appliances that enable administrators to collect telemetry from cloud-hosted firewalls, virtual routers, or load balancers. This allows organizations to maintain a consistent monitoring strategy across both private data centers and public cloud environments, supporting hybrid operations and workload mobility.

Ultimately, SNMP's role in virtualization environments lies in its ability to provide standardized, scalable, and vendor-neutral monitoring capabilities that extend across both physical and virtual infrastructure components. Its compatibility with a wide range of virtualization platforms, combined with its simplicity and efficiency, makes SNMP an essential tool for ensuring the operational health, security, and performance of modern virtualized environments. Whether used to monitor hypervisor health, virtual network traffic, VM resource consumption, or underlying storage systems, SNMP continues to empower administrators to manage increasingly complex and dynamic IT infrastructures with confidence and precision.

SNMP Security Basics

As one of the most widely implemented protocols for network management, SNMP plays a crucial role in monitoring and controlling devices such as routers, switches, firewalls, servers, and other networked equipment. However, its widespread use also makes it a target for security threats if not properly secured. SNMP security is a foundational aspect of protecting the integrity, availability, and confidentiality of management traffic across networks. Understanding SNMP security basics is critical for network administrators to ensure that sensitive data is not exposed and that network infrastructure cannot be tampered with by unauthorized users.

SNMP versions differ significantly in their approach to security. SNMPv1 and SNMPv2c were designed with simplicity and ease of implementation in mind but lacked robust security mechanisms. Both rely on community strings for authentication, which act as a form of password used to control access to SNMP agents on devices. Community strings are transmitted in plaintext, making them vulnerable to interception and sniffing attacks, especially when SNMP traffic traverses untrusted or unsecured network segments. Two common community strings used in SNMPv1 and SNMPv2c environments are public and private, where public typically grants read-only access and private provides read-write privileges. Using default or weak community strings presents a significant security risk, as attackers can easily exploit them to gather network information or make unauthorized changes to device configurations.

In contrast, SNMPv3 introduced comprehensive security improvements designed to address the shortcomings of earlier versions. The SNMPv3 User-based Security Model (USM) provides mechanisms for authentication, encryption, and message integrity. With SNMPv3, administrators can configure user accounts with defined security levels, enabling more granular control over who can access and modify network management information. The three primary security levels in SNMPv3 are noAuthNoPriv, which provides neither authentication nor encryption; authNoPriv, which adds authentication but no encryption; and authPriv, which offers both authentication and encryption, providing the highest level of protection.

Authentication in SNMPv3 is typically based on hash functions such as HMAC-MD5 or HMAC-SHA. When a manager sends a request to an agent, the authentication mechanism verifies that the message originates from a trusted user by validating the provided credentials. This prevents unauthorized entities from impersonating legitimate users. Encryption, on the other hand, secures SNMP traffic by encrypting the contents of messages using protocols such as DES or AES, protecting sensitive management data from eavesdropping. Message integrity ensures that SNMP packets have not been altered in transit by generating a message digest that is validated on receipt.

Implementing SNMPv3 security best practices is essential for protecting modern network environments. First, administrators should disable SNMPv1 and SNMPv2c where possible, migrating devices to SNMPv3 to take advantage of its enhanced security features. For legacy devices that only support older SNMP versions, the use of access control lists (ACLs) to restrict SNMP access to trusted management hosts is a minimum requirement. Administrators should also avoid using default community strings and instead configure complex, unique strings that are difficult to guess. Additionally, limiting SNMP access to specific IP ranges or management VLANs helps reduce the attack surface and prevents unauthorized users from querying or altering SNMP-exposed data.

Another fundamental aspect of SNMP security is managing access permissions carefully. SNMP provides read-only (RO) and read-write (RW) community strings or user accounts. The read-only role allows managers to query device information but prohibits them from making configuration changes. The read-write role permits both querying and modifying SNMP-managed objects, which can include critical settings such as interface states, routing tables, or system parameters. In most environments, the read-write role should be tightly controlled and limited to a small number of trusted administrators to prevent unauthorized or accidental configuration changes that could disrupt network operations.

Logging and monitoring SNMP activity also plays a key role in maintaining security. Administrators should configure devices to log SNMP queries, updates, and authentication failures. These logs can be forwarded to a centralized logging server or SIEM system, where they are analyzed for suspicious patterns or unauthorized access attempts. For example, multiple failed SNMPv3 authentication attempts could indicate a brute-force attack, while unusual spikes in SNMP write operations might suggest malicious activity. By closely monitoring SNMP activity, organizations can quickly detect and respond to potential security incidents.

Network segmentation is another strategy for improving SNMP security. By isolating management traffic on dedicated VLANs or separate out-of-band networks, organizations reduce the risk of SNMP traffic being intercepted or manipulated by unauthorized users. Combining network segmentation with encrypted SNMPv3 traffic creates a layered defense that strengthens the security posture of the network.

In addition to protecting SNMP itself, it is important to secure the broader network management ecosystem. SNMP managers, traps receivers, and network monitoring systems should be hardened to prevent exploitation. This includes securing operating systems, applying patches, enforcing strong authentication policies for user access, and configuring proper firewall rules to allow SNMP traffic only where necessary.

Many organizations also implement role-based access control (RBAC) in their SNMP management systems to define permissions based on user roles and responsibilities. This limits the exposure of sensitive SNMP data and control functions to only those who require them as part of their job duties. For example, a junior network technician might only be granted read-only access to specific device groups, while senior engineers have read-write permissions across the entire infrastructure.

Finally, periodic audits of SNMP configurations are critical for maintaining long-term security. Over time, as networks evolve and personnel change, community strings, SNMP users, and device configurations may become outdated or inconsistent with current security policies. Regular audits ensure that community strings and SNMPv3 user accounts are reviewed and updated, unused accounts are removed, and configurations remain aligned with industry best practices.

By following these SNMP security basics, organizations can significantly reduce the risks associated with using SNMP in their networks. While SNMP is an essential tool for managing and monitoring devices, its power also makes it a potential vector for attacks if left unsecured. Implementing strong authentication, encryption, access control, and monitoring practices ensures that SNMP continues to serve as a reliable and secure foundation for network management in today's increasingly complex and security-conscious IT environments.

SNMPv3: Authentication and Encryption

SNMPv3 introduced a comprehensive set of security features to address the shortcomings of earlier versions of the protocol. SNMPv1 and SNMPv2c were simple and widely adopted but lacked robust mechanisms for protecting the confidentiality, integrity, and authenticity of SNMP traffic. As networks expanded and became more complex, these limitations exposed critical infrastructure to risks such as unauthorized access, data tampering, and information leakage. SNMPv3 responded to these challenges by incorporating authentication and encryption capabilities, establishing itself as the secure alternative for managing and monitoring modern network environments.

One of the core components of SNMPv3 is its User-based Security Model (USM), which defines how users are authenticated and how messages are protected. Authentication in SNMPv3 ensures that SNMP managers and agents can verify the identity of the entities they are communicating with, preventing unauthorized users from impersonating legitimate devices or administrators. This is achieved using cryptographic hash functions such as HMAC-MD5 or HMAC-SHA, which generate unique message digests based on the content of SNMP packets and shared secret keys. When an SNMP manager sends a request to an agent, the agent verifies the authenticity of the request by calculating its own hash and comparing it to the one received. If they match, the message is considered valid.

The authentication process in SNMPv3 prevents attackers from injecting malicious SNMP commands into the network, such as unauthorized SNMP Set requests that could modify device configurations or disable critical interfaces. It also protects against replay attacks, where an attacker intercepts and retransmits previously captured SNMP packets to cause unintended actions. Each SNMPv3 message includes a unique engine ID, time stamp, and sequence number to ensure that it is processed once and only once, further reinforcing the integrity of the communication.

In addition to authentication, SNMPv3 offers encryption through the use of privacy protocols such as DES (Data Encryption Standard) and AES (Advanced Encryption Standard). Encryption protects SNMP traffic from being intercepted and read by unauthorized parties. Without encryption, SNMP messages—including sensitive information like community strings, configuration parameters, and device status—are transmitted in plaintext, making them vulnerable to eavesdropping. By enabling SNMPv3's privacy features, administrators can ensure that SNMP packets are encrypted, preserving the confidentiality of the data as it traverses potentially insecure or shared networks.

The combination of authentication and encryption in SNMPv3 is referred to as the authPriv security level. SNMPv3 allows administrators to configure different security levels based on organizational requirements. The lowest level, noAuthNoPriv, offers neither authentication nor encryption and is typically reserved for environments where security is not a concern, such as isolated lab networks. The authNoPriv level provides authentication without encryption, offering protection against unauthorized access but leaving data exposed to interception. The highest level, authPriv, provides both authentication and encryption, making it the recommended configuration for production environments where data confidentiality and integrity are critical.

When configuring SNMPv3, administrators define user accounts with specific authentication and privacy parameters. Each user is associated with an authentication protocol, an authentication passphrase, an encryption protocol, and an encryption passphrase. Best practices dictate that these passphrases should be strong, unique, and updated regularly to prevent unauthorized access. The use of AES, with its stronger encryption capabilities compared to DES, is highly recommended, especially in environments where regulatory compliance standards require robust data protection measures.

SNMPv3 also enhances access control by supporting fine-grained permissions for different user accounts. Administrators can create multiple SNMPv3 users with distinct access rights, limiting who can perform read-only operations versus who can issue read-write commands. For example, a network engineer might be granted a user account with permissions to modify device configurations via SNMP Set requests, while a junior technician may only have read access to retrieve monitoring data. This level of control minimizes the risk of accidental or malicious changes to network devices and helps organizations enforce the principle of least privilege.

The security benefits of SNMPv3 are particularly relevant in large, distributed networks where SNMP messages often cross multiple segments and traverse shared infrastructure. In such environments, relying on SNMPv1 or SNMPv2c with plaintext community strings exposes critical management data to interception and tampering. By adopting SNMPv3's authentication and encryption mechanisms, organizations can safeguard SNMP traffic even when it crosses unsecured segments, such as public or semi-public network links.

Moreover, SNMPv3's security model is essential for meeting compliance requirements in regulated industries. Frameworks such as

PCI DSS, HIPAA, and GDPR mandate strong protections for sensitive data and require that management traffic be encrypted when traversing networks. SNMPv3's support for secure authentication and encryption allows organizations to align their network management practices with these regulatory standards, reducing the risk of compliance violations and data breaches.

SNMPv3 authentication and encryption also integrate smoothly with broader network security strategies. When combined with access control lists (ACLs) that limit which IP addresses can initiate SNMP sessions, network segmentation that isolates management traffic, and centralized logging that captures authentication attempts and SNMP activities, SNMPv3 contributes to a layered defense-in-depth model. These combined controls reduce the likelihood of successful attacks and ensure that network management systems remain resilient in the face of evolving security threats.

Another advantage of SNMPv3's security model is its ability to support secure trap and inform messages. Traps and informs are critical for real-time network monitoring, as they provide alerts about fault conditions, threshold breaches, and other important events. In earlier SNMP versions, traps were sent without encryption or authentication, making them susceptible to spoofing or interception. With SNMPv3, traps and informs can be configured to require both authentication and encryption, ensuring that alerts originate from trusted sources and are protected during transit.

Despite its security advantages, SNMPv3 is sometimes underutilized due to the perception that it is more complex to configure compared to its predecessors. However, the investment in configuring SNMPv3 properly pays dividends in risk reduction and operational reliability. Network administrators are encouraged to familiarize themselves with SNMPv3's configuration syntax, including setting up SNMP engine IDs, defining user accounts, and testing communication between SNMP managers and agents to ensure secure connectivity.

SNMPv3's introduction of authentication and encryption represents a significant evolution in the protocol's maturity and its ability to meet the security demands of modern networks. As cyber threats become increasingly sophisticated, securing network management protocols is no longer optional but a necessity. SNMPv3 offers the tools required to protect the confidentiality, integrity, and authenticity of network management traffic, ensuring that organizations can monitor and control their infrastructure without exposing themselves to undue security risks.

Configuring SNMP Access Control

Configuring SNMP access control is a critical task in securing network management systems and protecting the sensitive information exchanged between SNMP managers and agents. SNMP allows administrators to remotely monitor and control network devices such as routers, switches, servers, firewalls, and storage systems. However, without proper access control measures, SNMP can be exploited by unauthorized users to gain insight into network infrastructure or make disruptive changes to device configurations. Access control mechanisms help limit who can access SNMP agents and what level of permissions they have, safeguarding the management plane of the network.

SNMP access control differs across SNMP versions, but the goal is always to restrict and define who has the authority to perform SNMP operations. In SNMPv1 and SNMPv2c, the primary method of access control is through the use of community strings. These are plaintext passwords that act as a shared secret between the SNMP manager and agent. Typically, there are two community strings: one for read-only access and another for read-write access. The read-only community string allows the SNMP manager to query the agent for information but prevents any configuration changes, while the read-write community string enables both monitoring and modifications to the managed device.

The use of community strings in SNMPv1 and SNMPv2c presents several security concerns, especially since they are transmitted without encryption. As a result, administrators must configure community strings to be long, complex, and non-default to avoid easy guessing or interception. It is common to encounter legacy devices configured with default community strings such as "public" and "private," which can be exploited by attackers to gain unauthorized access. To mitigate these risks, administrators should always replace default community strings with strong, unique values and restrict SNMP access to trusted IP addresses or management subnets using access control lists (ACLs) at the device or network layer.

SNMPv3 introduced more advanced access control capabilities through its User-based Security Model (USM). Rather than relying solely on community strings, SNMPv3 allows administrators to create user accounts with different authentication and encryption settings. Each user can be assigned specific security levels: noAuthNoPriv, authNoPriv, or authPriv, depending on the desired level of protection. This allows administrators to implement more granular access control by defining which users can perform specific SNMP operations and what security mechanisms are required.

Configuring SNMPv3 access control starts with defining SNMP engine IDs and creating user accounts on the managed devices. Each SNMPv3 user is associated with an authentication protocol, such as MD5 or SHA, and optionally with a privacy protocol, such as DES or AES. For instance, a user might be created with authPriv settings, requiring both authentication and encryption before they can communicate with the SNMP agent. By creating different user profiles for network operators, system administrators, or monitoring tools, organizations can limit SNMP operations to only those who have a legitimate need to perform them.

SNMPv3 also supports the concept of views, groups, and access policies as part of the View-based Access Control Model (VACM). Views define which portions of the MIB tree a user is allowed to access, while groups organize users based on common access rights. Access policies link users or groups to specific views and determine whether they have read-only, read-write, or notify (trap generation) permissions. For example, an administrator could configure a view that allows a user to access only interface-related MIB objects, while restricting access to system configuration objects. This granular control helps enforce the principle of least privilege and reduces the attack surface by exposing only necessary information to each user or system.

In many network environments, administrators also rely on network-layer access control mechanisms to supplement SNMP's built-in controls. Devices can be configured with ACLs to permit SNMP traffic only from specific IP addresses or management networks. By limiting SNMP traffic to known management stations, NOC centers, or monitoring servers, organizations can prevent unauthorized hosts from querying or altering SNMP data. This is especially important in large-scale or distributed environments where devices are accessible over WAN or public networks.

In addition to configuring ACLs, best practices recommend isolating SNMP management traffic from production data traffic through the use of management VLANs or out-of-band management networks. Segregating SNMP traffic reduces the risk of interception or tampering by limiting its exposure to trusted network segments. When combined with SNMPv3 encryption and authentication, this layered approach significantly enhances the security of SNMP operations.

Another important element of configuring SNMP access control is securing SNMP traps and informs. SNMP agents often send traps to inform SNMP managers of significant events such as hardware failures, link status changes, or security incidents. In SNMPv1 and SNMPv2c, traps can be sent without authentication, making them vulnerable to spoofing. SNMPv3 enables secure trap generation through the use of user accounts with authentication and encryption settings. Administrators should configure agents to send traps to designated SNMP managers that have been authorized via SNMPv3 user accounts, ensuring that alerts are both genuine and protected from tampering during transmission.

Centralized monitoring platforms and network management systems (NMS) play a key role in enforcing SNMP access control policies. These systems should be configured to authenticate to SNMP agents using secure SNMPv3 credentials and to comply with the access views and permissions established on managed devices. Additionally, SNMP activity should be logged and reviewed regularly. Logs of SNMP queries, authentication attempts, and configuration changes provide valuable insight into how SNMP is being used and can help identify unauthorized or anomalous behavior.

Finally, administrators should conduct periodic audits of SNMP configurations across all managed devices. Over time, organizations may experience personnel changes, infrastructure growth, or policy updates that render some SNMP user accounts, community strings, or ACLs obsolete or misaligned with current security standards. Regular audits ensure that SNMP configurations remain consistent, that unused or legacy accounts are removed, and that access controls are enforced uniformly across the network.

Effective SNMP access control is essential for protecting the management layer of modern networks. By combining SNMPv3's advanced security features with strict network-layer access controls, user permissions, and traffic segmentation strategies, organizations can maintain the integrity, confidentiality, and availability of SNMP-based management systems. Careful and consistent configuration of SNMP access control ensures that network operations are secure, reliable, and resilient against internal and external threats.

SNMP Community Strings and Their Risks

SNMP community strings have long been a fundamental component of network management, particularly in SNMPv1 and SNMPv2c environments. These community strings act as simple forms of authentication, functioning much like passwords to control access to SNMP-enabled devices. However, their simplicity and the lack of robust security mechanisms in older SNMP versions have introduced significant risks for organizations relying on SNMP for network monitoring and management. Understanding the role of community strings, how they work, and the vulnerabilities associated with them is essential for mitigating threats to network infrastructure.

In SNMPv1 and SNMPv2c, community strings are transmitted as part of SNMP requests from the manager to the agent. The two most common types of community strings are read-only and read-write. A read-only community string allows the SNMP manager to query the device and retrieve monitoring data such as system uptime, interface statistics, CPU usage, or memory status. A read-write community string, on the other hand, grants the SNMP manager permission to modify certain device parameters using SNMP Set requests. These modifications can include enabling or disabling interfaces, changing routing configurations, or adjusting system settings.

The primary risk associated with SNMP community strings stems from the fact that they are transmitted in plaintext over the network. Without any encryption or hashing, these strings can be easily captured by an attacker performing a packet-sniffing attack on the same network segment. Once intercepted, an attacker can use the compromised community string to gain unauthorized access to network devices. If a read-write community string is compromised, the threat escalates significantly, as the attacker can actively modify device configurations, potentially disrupting services, redirecting traffic, or degrading network performance.

A common and dangerous practice in many organizations is the use of default community strings. Many network devices are shipped with factory-set community strings, typically labeled as public for read-only access and private for read-write access. If administrators fail to change these defaults during the deployment process, it leaves the infrastructure exposed to unauthorized access. Attackers often scan networks for SNMP-enabled devices and attempt common community strings as part of automated attacks or reconnaissance efforts. Finding devices that still use default strings is a low-effort, high-reward opportunity for malicious actors to gain visibility into network topology and performance metrics.

Another risk related to community strings is their widespread re-use across multiple devices. In large-scale networks, it is not uncommon for administrators to configure the same community string on numerous devices to simplify management and reduce the operational overhead of managing unique credentials for each device. While this approach may streamline some aspects of configuration, it creates a single point of failure. If one device is compromised and the community string is exposed, all other devices using the same string are also vulnerable.

Community strings also lack granularity in terms of access control. Unlike modern authentication models, SNMPv1 and SNMPv2c community strings do not provide user-level access differentiation.

Any user or system possessing the correct community string is granted the full set of permissions associated with that string, regardless of their role or intent. This creates an environment where privileges cannot be effectively segregated or audited at an individual level, making it more difficult to apply the principle of least privilege or to track who performed specific SNMP operations on the network.

Misconfigured SNMP agents further exacerbate the risks of community strings. For example, if SNMP agents are inadvertently configured with open access to the entire internet or to untrusted network segments, attackers located outside of the organization's internal network can remotely exploit vulnerable devices. Misconfiguration can also include leaving SNMP enabled on devices where it is not required, thereby increasing the number of potential attack surfaces unnecessarily.

The lack of encryption and weak authentication mechanisms associated with SNMP community strings have prompted security best practices aimed at reducing their associated risks. At a minimum, administrators should always replace default community strings with strong, complex alternatives that are difficult to guess. Community strings should consist of a mix of upper and lowercase letters, numbers, and special characters, and should avoid dictionary words or easily guessable phrases.

In addition to using strong community strings, administrators should implement access control lists (ACLs) on network devices to restrict which IP addresses or subnets are permitted to query SNMP agents. By limiting SNMP access to known management stations or trusted networks, organizations can reduce the likelihood of unauthorized access attempts. Another common best practice is to disable SNMP entirely on devices or interfaces where it is not needed, minimizing the attack surface.

Network segmentation also plays an important role in mitigating risks associated with SNMP community strings. By isolating management traffic on separate VLANs or dedicated management networks, organizations can reduce the exposure of SNMP packets to general user traffic or untrusted systems. Combined with firewall rules and ACLs, this segmentation provides an additional layer of protection for SNMP communications.

While SNMPv1 and SNMPv2c remain widely used due to their simplicity and broad compatibility, organizations are encouraged to migrate to SNMPv3 whenever possible. SNMPv3 introduces a much more secure user-based authentication model along with support for encryption and message integrity, effectively addressing many of the security gaps inherent in earlier versions. SNMPv3 eliminates the reliance on community strings in favor of user accounts with configurable access permissions and secure communication channels.

However, for organizations that must continue to use SNMPv1 or SNMPv2c due to legacy systems or vendor limitations, compensating controls become even more critical. In addition to strong strings, ACLs, and network segmentation, continuous monitoring of SNMP activity through centralized logging and SIEM systems can help detect unauthorized access attempts. Unusual patterns, such as SNMP requests originating from untrusted IP ranges or an increase in SNMP Set operations, may indicate that a community string has been compromised.

Periodic audits of SNMP configurations across all network devices are also recommended to ensure that community strings follow current security policies and best practices. During these audits, administrators should verify that no default or weak community strings remain in use, that SNMP access is appropriately restricted, and that devices are not unnecessarily exposed to external or untrusted networks.

While SNMP community strings have long been a fundamental part of network management, their limitations and associated risks cannot be ignored. Without proper security controls, these simple authentication mechanisms can expose critical infrastructure to unauthorized access and malicious activity. Organizations must take proactive steps to secure SNMP implementations, balancing the need for efficient network management with the imperative to protect sensitive systems and data from evolving threats.

SNMP and Role-Based Access Control (RBAC)

The integration of SNMP with Role-Based Access Control (RBAC) represents a powerful method for enhancing security and operational efficiency in network management. SNMP has traditionally provided mechanisms for querying and managing network devices through operations such as Get, Set, and Trap. However, without a framework to differentiate permissions based on user roles, SNMP implementations—especially in earlier versions like SNMPv1 and SNMPv2c—can expose organizations to unnecessary risks. The addition of RBAC principles to SNMPv3 strengthens the protocol by enabling administrators to define clear access rights, limit the actions users can perform, and enforce the principle of least privilege.

RBAC is a security model in which user permissions are assigned according to predefined roles rather than individual user accounts. Each role corresponds to a specific set of responsibilities within the organization, and users are granted permissions based on the role they fulfill. This model simplifies access control, improves auditability, and reduces the risk of privilege misuse or accidental configuration errors. Within the context of SNMPv3, RBAC allows network administrators to create user profiles with specific permissions over SNMP-managed objects, providing more granular control over device management operations.

SNMPv3 natively supports RBAC-like functionality through its View-based Access Control Model (VACM). VACM introduces three main components: views, groups, and access policies. Views define subsets of the Management Information Base (MIB) tree, specifying which objects can be accessed by certain users. Groups are collections of SNMPv3 users who share common access requirements. Access policies bind these groups to specific views and define the allowed SNMP operations, such as read-only, read-write, or notify (trap-related) permissions.

For example, in a large enterprise network, a junior network technician might be assigned to a group that has read-only access to interface status and system uptime objects within the MIB. This technician can monitor the operational state of devices but cannot make any configuration changes. In contrast, a senior network engineer may belong to a group with read-write permissions for a broader set of MIB objects, including those that control VLAN configurations, interface states, and routing parameters. A third group may be created for security analysts who only need access to SNMP notifications related to security events or system faults, without any read or write permissions to the MIB.

This level of granularity offers significant security benefits. It ensures that users only have access to the information and functionality necessary to perform their job roles. By limiting access to critical SNMP operations such as Set requests, which can modify device configurations, organizations can prevent unauthorized or accidental changes that could disrupt network services. At the same time, providing read-only access to specific portions of the MIB allows monitoring and troubleshooting activities to continue unhindered.

RBAC within SNMPv3 is also valuable for organizations that operate in regulated industries or under strict compliance mandates. Regulatory frameworks often require organizations to implement strict controls over who can access and modify sensitive systems and data. By aligning SNMP access permissions with defined roles and responsibilities, organizations can demonstrate adherence to security best practices and compliance requirements, such as those outlined by PCI DSS, HIPAA, or ISO/IEC 27001. The ability to audit which users have access to specific SNMP operations and MIB views provides accountability and simplifies compliance reporting.

In addition to controlling access to MIB objects, RBAC in SNMP environments can help enforce operational boundaries between teams. For example, in a shared infrastructure where multiple teams manage different segments of the network, each team can be granted access to only their respective device groups or network segments. SNMPv3's VACM model allows administrators to create views that limit access to devices or object identifiers that fall within specific IP address ranges or organizational units. This segmentation helps reduce the likelihood of operational conflicts and enhances security by preventing users from viewing or modifying devices outside their area of responsibility.

Configuring RBAC within SNMPv3 requires careful planning and implementation. Administrators must first analyze the organizational structure to define the appropriate roles and responsibilities. Once roles are identified, SNMPv3 users are created and grouped according to their functional areas. Views are then defined to map which parts of the MIB tree each group can access. Finally, access policies are applied to enforce these permissions.

For example, in a data center environment, a facilities team may be given read-only access to MIB objects related to environmental sensors and power distribution units (PDUs), while the network engineering team has read-write permissions for networking devices. The security operations team might have access only to trap notifications related to firewall status, intrusion detection systems, or security event logs. This role-based structure ensures that each team has access to only the information that pertains to their operational scope.

RBAC implementation in SNMPv3 also improves the incident response process. During security incidents or network outages, it is critical to control who has the authority to make changes to the network. By limiting write permissions to senior personnel or incident response teams, RBAC helps prevent unauthorized or uncoordinated actions that could exacerbate the situation. Furthermore, SNMP audit logs can track the specific users and roles associated with SNMP operations, supporting forensic investigations and post-incident reviews.

Organizations can further enhance RBAC by integrating SNMPv3 with centralized identity and access management (IAM) solutions or directory services, streamlining user authentication and role assignment. While SNMPv3 does not natively integrate with external authentication systems like RADIUS or TACACS+, many SNMP managers and network devices offer hybrid models where SNMP authentication is combined with centralized user management systems to enforce consistent role-based permissions across both SNMP and other management protocols.

RBAC also supports operational efficiency by simplifying user management. Instead of configuring permissions on a per-user basis, administrators manage roles and group memberships. When personnel changes occur, such as onboarding new staff or reassigning duties, administrators only need to update the user's group membership without modifying individual device configurations. This centralized approach reduces administrative overhead, minimizes the risk of misconfigurations, and supports scalability in large enterprise networks.

The incorporation of RBAC principles into SNMPv3 access control significantly strengthens the security and governance of network management operations. By defining roles, segmenting access to sensitive SNMP-managed objects, and enforcing the principle of least privilege, organizations can reduce the risk of unauthorized actions, improve operational workflows, and meet regulatory compliance demands more effectively. In complex network environments where multiple teams and stakeholders rely on SNMP for visibility and control, RBAC ensures that access to critical infrastructure remains secure, structured, and aligned with business and security objectives.

SNMP Hardening Best Practices

Securing SNMP implementations is a critical task for network administrators tasked with protecting infrastructure management protocols. SNMP is widely used to monitor and control network devices such as routers, switches, servers, and firewalls, but if left improperly configured or unsecured, it becomes a potential vector for information leakage and unauthorized access. Hardening SNMP environments is essential for maintaining the confidentiality, integrity, and availability of network management operations. Applying best practices for SNMP hardening helps to ensure that organizations minimize exposure to common threats while preserving the efficiency and functionality of their network monitoring processes.

One of the foundational SNMP hardening practices is to avoid using SNMPv1 and SNMPv2c whenever possible. Both of these earlier versions transmit community strings in plaintext and lack any form of built-in encryption or message authentication. This makes them highly susceptible to eavesdropping, man-in-the-middle attacks, and unauthorized access. Organizations that continue to rely on SNMPv1 or SNMPv2c for compatibility reasons must apply strict access controls to mitigate their inherent weaknesses. However, migrating to SNMPv3 should be the priority, as SNMPv3 offers support for secure authentication, encryption, and message integrity verification.

Once SNMPv3 is implemented, administrators should enforce its strongest security settings. SNMPv3 allows for the creation of user accounts with different security levels, including noAuthNoPriv, authNoPriv, and authPriv. The recommended setting for most production environments is authPriv, which provides both authentication and encryption. Authentication mechanisms, such as HMAC-SHA, ensure that only verified users can access SNMP agents, while encryption protocols like AES protect SNMP communications from interception and tampering. Weak encryption methods such as DES should be avoided whenever possible, as they no longer meet modern security standards.

Another key SNMP hardening practice involves the management of SNMP community strings and user accounts. In environments where SNMPv1 or SNMPv2c must still be used, administrators should replace default community strings with complex and unique values. Default strings such as public and private are well-known and commonly exploited by attackers during automated scans. Community strings should consist of randomized combinations of uppercase and lowercase letters, numbers, and special characters, and they should be changed regularly to prevent reuse over time. SNMPv3 user accounts should also be configured with strong passphrases and follow the organization's broader password management policies.

Restricting SNMP access to trusted sources is another essential component of hardening. Access control lists (ACLs) should be implemented on all SNMP-enabled devices to limit which IP addresses or subnets are allowed to query SNMP agents. Only trusted management servers, network operations centers, or monitoring systems should have SNMP access. SNMP traffic should not be accessible from general user networks or external networks unless explicitly required and tightly controlled. Additionally, limiting SNMP to specific management VLANs or out-of-band management networks further reduces exposure by segmenting it from production traffic.

Device-level hardening is equally important when securing SNMP. SNMP agents should only be enabled on interfaces where management access is needed. For example, enabling SNMP on external-facing interfaces or interfaces exposed to public networks is a significant security risk. In most cases, SNMP should only be active on internal interfaces accessible from secured management networks. Disabling SNMP on unnecessary interfaces minimizes the available attack surface and reduces the risk of unauthorized access.

The principle of least privilege should guide SNMP permissions. SNMPv3, with its View-based Access Control Model (VACM), allows administrators to define user roles with specific access rights to different parts of the MIB hierarchy. Read-write permissions should be granted sparingly and only to trusted users who require the ability to modify device configurations. Most monitoring systems only require read-only access to gather telemetry and performance data. By limiting write access to a small group of authorized administrators, organizations can prevent accidental or malicious configuration changes through SNMP Set operations.

Hardening SNMP also involves securing SNMP trap and inform configurations. Traps are used to send asynchronous event notifications from SNMP agents to managers. In SNMPv1 and SNMPv2c, traps are sent without authentication or encryption, making them susceptible to spoofing or interception. SNMPv3 supports authenticated and encrypted traps and informs, which should be used to ensure that alerts are genuine and protected from tampering. Additionally, trap destinations should be explicitly defined, and only authorized SNMP managers should be allowed to receive traps from network devices.

Logging and monitoring SNMP activity is another best practice to enhance situational awareness and security. SNMP agents and management platforms should generate detailed logs of SNMP queries, configuration changes, and authentication attempts. These logs should be forwarded to a centralized logging or SIEM system, where they can be analyzed for suspicious activity. Unusual patterns, such as repeated authentication failures or unexpected SNMP Set requests, may indicate brute-force attempts or insider threats. By maintaining comprehensive logs, organizations can detect and respond to security incidents more quickly.

Another key aspect of SNMP hardening is reducing the overall number of SNMP-enabled devices in the environment. Conducting regular audits to identify devices where SNMP is no longer necessary helps minimize unnecessary exposure. Devices that are no longer managed via SNMP, or where SNMP functionality has been replaced by modern APIs or telemetry protocols, should have SNMP disabled altogether. Removing unused SNMP services is a simple but effective way to reduce potential entry points for attackers.

Organizations should also ensure that firmware and software on SNMP-enabled devices are kept up to date. Vendors frequently release patches and updates that address vulnerabilities related to SNMP implementations. Outdated device firmware may contain exploitable SNMP-related flaws that can be leveraged by attackers to gain unauthorized access or disrupt network management operations. Maintaining a robust patch management process is essential to reducing the risk of exploitation.

In environments with highly sensitive systems or strict regulatory requirements, SNMP traffic should be encrypted at the network layer in addition to using SNMPv3's built-in security. Implementing IPsec tunnels or SSL/TLS-based VPNs for management traffic further enhances the confidentiality and integrity of SNMP communications. This layered approach is particularly beneficial when SNMP messages must traverse untrusted networks or when compliance mandates require end-to-end encryption.

SNMP hardening best practices should be integrated into the broader network security strategy, ensuring alignment with firewall configurations, identity and access management policies, and incident response procedures. Regular security assessments and penetration tests should include SNMP exposure as part of their scope, verifying that access controls, encryption settings, and monitoring systems are functioning as intended.

By following these SNMP hardening best practices, organizations can significantly reduce the risks associated with SNMP-based network management. While SNMP remains a critical tool for visibility and control, securing its implementation is paramount to protecting network infrastructure from evolving cyber threats. A well-hardened SNMP environment supports operational reliability, enhances compliance posture, and ensures that network management systems remain resilient and secure.

Detecting and Mitigating SNMP Attacks

SNMP, as one of the most widely used protocols for network management, offers administrators a powerful tool for monitoring and controlling devices such as routers, switches, firewalls, and servers. However, its widespread adoption and simplicity also make it an attractive target for attackers. Without proper security measures, SNMP implementations can become vulnerable to a range of attacks that exploit weak authentication, lack of encryption, and misconfigurations. Detecting and mitigating SNMP attacks is crucial to maintaining the integrity, availability, and confidentiality of network infrastructure. Understanding common SNMP attack vectors and applying appropriate countermeasures helps organizations defend against potential exploits and ensure secure network operations.

One of the most common types of SNMP attacks is unauthorized access due to weak or default community strings. In SNMPv1 and SNMPv2c, community strings are used as passwords to control access to SNMP agents on devices. However, these community strings are often transmitted in plaintext, making them vulnerable to interception by attackers. Default community strings such as "public" (for read-only access) and "private" (for read-write access) are widely known and frequently left unchanged, making it easy for attackers to gain access to network devices through brute-force attacks or simple reconnaissance. Once attackers discover these community strings, they can query sensitive information from SNMP-enabled devices or, in the worst case, make configuration changes that disrupt network operations.

One effective way to detect unauthorized access attempts is by monitoring SNMP query logs for unusual patterns. A sudden increase in SNMP requests or requests coming from unauthorized IP addresses could be a sign that an attacker is attempting to exploit weak community strings or engage in reconnaissance. Anomalous access to devices, especially when devices that should not be accessible via SNMP are queried, may indicate an attack in progress. Additionally, administrators should configure SNMP to limit access to trusted IP ranges, ensuring that only authorized network management systems or users can query SNMP agents. Disabling SNMP on devices where it is not necessary and changing default community strings to strong, unique passwords are essential measures in preventing unauthorized access.

Another prevalent SNMP attack is the SNMP DoS (Denial of Service) attack. This type of attack typically involves overwhelming an SNMP-enabled device with a flood of SNMP requests, often with the goal of exhausting system resources such as CPU or memory. The attacker may send an excessive number of SNMP queries or exploit SNMP traps to trigger excessive processing, causing the targeted device to crash, freeze, or become unresponsive. To detect this kind of attack, network monitoring systems can track the frequency and volume of SNMP requests to identify spikes that may indicate a DoS attack. Implementing rate limiting and filtering SNMP traffic based on IP addresses and networks can help mitigate the risk of DoS attacks by reducing the ability of malicious actors to flood devices with requests.

Another major concern is SNMP-based man-in-the-middle (MitM) attacks. In these attacks, an attacker intercepts and potentially alters SNMP messages between the manager and the agent, manipulating network configuration or collecting sensitive data. Since SNMPv1 and SNMPv2c transmit community strings and data in plaintext, these attacks are especially easy to execute in unprotected network environments. To detect MitM attacks, administrators should monitor for signs of traffic interception, such as unexpected network latency or changes in traffic flow patterns. One of the most effective ways to prevent MitM attacks is to implement SNMPv3, which supports encrypted communication and message integrity verification, making it significantly more resistant to interception or tampering. By using SNMPv3 with both authentication and encryption, the integrity and confidentiality of SNMP traffic are maintained, reducing the risk of successful MitM attacks.

SNMP spoofing is another type of attack in which an attacker impersonates an SNMP manager or agent to send false data or commands to network devices. In an SNMP spoofing attack, the attacker may send an SNMP trap to a management system, pretending to be a legitimate device, or respond to SNMP queries with false information. This can mislead administrators or automated systems into believing that a device is operating normally when, in fact, it is compromised or malfunctioning. Detecting SNMP spoofing typically involves monitoring the source of SNMP traps and verifying that incoming messages match the expected SNMP manager or device. One of the key mitigation strategies is to configure SNMP to only accept requests and traps from trusted, pre-defined IP addresses. Furthermore, enabling encryption and authentication in SNMPv3 ensures that traps and responses are validated and not easily spoofed.

In addition to these specific attack vectors, SNMP attacks can also be exacerbated by poor configuration practices, such as leaving SNMP enabled on devices that do not need it, using weak community strings, or not restricting SNMP access to specific subnets or management networks. To mitigate these risks, administrators must adopt a proactive approach to SNMP security by regularly auditing configurations, removing unnecessary SNMP functionality, and ensuring that strong authentication and encryption protocols are used. Moreover, periodic vulnerability assessments, penetration testing, and security audits should include SNMP systems to identify potential weaknesses and apply appropriate hardening measures.

One best practice in mitigating SNMP attacks is to use network segmentation. By isolating management traffic from general user and data traffic, organizations can protect SNMP traffic from being exposed to untrusted or public networks. This can be achieved by creating dedicated management VLANs or using out-of-band management channels that are separate from production network traffic. In addition, firewalls and access control lists (ACLs) should be configured to limit SNMP traffic to only authorized IP addresses and networks. This reduces the likelihood of external attacks from exploiting SNMP vulnerabilities and accessing critical network devices.

Network intrusion detection and prevention systems (IDPS) can also be configured to detect SNMP-specific attacks. These systems can flag unusual SNMP traffic patterns, such as a high number of requests from unknown IP addresses, attempts to access unauthorized MIB objects, or signs of SNMP DoS attacks. Integrating SNMP monitoring with an SIEM (Security Information and Event Management) system can further enhance visibility into SNMP-related threats by aggregating logs and alerting administrators to potential security incidents in real-time.

Finally, educating network administrators and security personnel about SNMP vulnerabilities and best practices is crucial in building a strong defense against SNMP-based attacks. Regular training on SNMP security, secure configuration, and attack detection techniques empowers teams to recognize and respond to threats promptly. Documenting SNMP security policies and incorporating them into the organization's broader security framework ensures consistency in protecting network management systems.

SNMP is an essential tool for network management, but its inherent vulnerabilities require constant attention and security hardening. By understanding the risks associated with SNMP and applying a layered defense strategy—combining strong authentication, encryption, traffic filtering, network segmentation, and real-time monitoring—organizations can significantly reduce their exposure to SNMP attacks. With careful planning, proactive configuration, and continuous vigilance, SNMP can remain a secure and reliable protocol for managing modern network infrastructures.

SNMP and Network Segmentation

Network segmentation is a critical security practice that involves dividing a network into smaller, more manageable segments or subnets to control traffic flow, enhance performance, and improve security. When it comes to managing and monitoring network devices, SNMP is an invaluable protocol that allows administrators to remotely query devices for performance data, configuration settings, and status updates. However, when not properly segmented, SNMP traffic can expose sensitive network information to malicious actors and increase the potential for unauthorized access. By combining SNMP with effective network segmentation, organizations can significantly reduce the attack surface and protect their network infrastructure from a wide array of security threats.

The integration of SNMP and network segmentation provides a layered defense that ensures network management data is kept separate from general network traffic, thus enhancing both performance and security. SNMP, by its nature, requires access to network devices such as routers, switches, firewalls, and servers. If SNMP traffic is allowed to traverse unsegmented network environments, it can be exposed to unauthorized users or attackers who might gain access to critical infrastructure data. By segmenting the network, administrators can isolate SNMP traffic to trusted management networks or VLANs (Virtual Local Area Networks), which reduces the risk of eavesdropping, tampering, and other malicious activities.

One of the main advantages of combining SNMP with network segmentation is that it prevents unauthorized access to network management traffic. Without segmentation, SNMP packets, including potentially sensitive information such as device configurations, performance metrics, and error messages, could be exposed to the broader network. Attackers who gain access to the network could sniff SNMP traffic and collect community strings or other sensitive information. Through network segmentation, SNMP traffic is isolated from the rest of the network, allowing only authorized devices and management servers to interact with SNMP-enabled devices. This is especially important in large-scale environments where the network is exposed to various user devices and untrusted systems that could serve as entry points for attacks.

Another benefit of network segmentation in SNMP management is the ability to implement more stringent access control measures. By creating dedicated management VLANs or isolated management networks, administrators can ensure that only specific devices, such as network monitoring systems and servers, are able to communicate with SNMP agents. Network segmentation can also be coupled with firewalls and access control lists (ACLs) that limit which IP addresses or subnets are allowed to send SNMP requests to network devices. This greatly reduces the potential for unauthorized users or systems to access SNMP data, ensuring that only trusted network management resources can query and interact with SNMP agents.

Segmenting the network also improves performance by reducing the amount of SNMP traffic that must be handled by each network device. In large enterprise networks, SNMP polling can generate a significant amount of traffic, especially when hundreds or thousands of devices are being monitored. By isolating SNMP traffic within a dedicated management network or VLAN, network congestion is minimized, and network devices can focus on handling critical traffic without being overloaded by SNMP queries. This enhances the efficiency of both network devices and SNMP-based monitoring systems, enabling faster response times and improved visibility into network health.

Furthermore, network segmentation enhances the security of SNMP-based communications by limiting the scope of potential attack vectors. For example, if a device within an untrusted segment is compromised, the attacker would only have access to the segment where the device resides and not to the entire network or management systems. Isolating management traffic ensures that even if an attacker gains access to one segment of the network, they cannot easily escalate their privileges or pivot to critical network infrastructure. In addition, network segmentation can restrict SNMP access to certain groups of devices, reducing the attack surface further and making it more difficult for attackers to move laterally across the network.

When combining SNMP with network segmentation, encryption becomes a critical consideration. While SNMPv3 provides built-in encryption and authentication mechanisms to secure SNMP traffic, it is still important to consider encryption at the network layer as an additional security measure. Encrypting SNMP traffic between network management stations and managed devices ensures that even if an attacker is able to intercept SNMP packets, they will not be able to read or modify the data. This can be achieved through IPsec or SSL/TLS-based VPNs, which create secure communication channels for SNMP traffic, protecting it from interception while it traverses untrusted network segments.

For large, distributed networks, implementing SNMP and network segmentation requires careful planning and configuration. Network administrators need to identify which devices require SNMP access and determine the optimal placement of management systems. Dedicated management VLANs should be configured to route SNMP traffic separately from regular data traffic, ensuring that monitoring and management tasks do not interfere with user traffic or other network operations. It is also important to ensure that SNMP traffic is properly segregated using VLAN tags or similar technologies to prevent unauthorized devices from accessing the management network.

While SNMP is a powerful tool for network management, it is only as secure as the infrastructure around it. Using SNMP in combination with network segmentation enhances security by limiting exposure to potential attacks and ensuring that sensitive network management data is not easily accessible to unauthorized users. It is essential to follow best practices in network segmentation to ensure that management traffic is properly isolated, encrypted, and secured. Network segmentation not only prevents unauthorized access but also improves the overall performance and resilience of SNMP-based monitoring systems.

One important aspect of network segmentation for SNMP is ensuring that it is part of an overarching network security strategy. Segmentation should be implemented in conjunction with other security controls, such as firewalls, intrusion detection systems (IDS), and intrusion prevention systems (IPS). This multi-layered approach provides comprehensive protection for SNMP traffic and network management systems. Additionally, it is essential to regularly audit the network segmentation architecture to ensure that it aligns with evolving security policies and that no vulnerabilities are introduced as the network grows or changes.

The combination of SNMP and network segmentation is an effective way to improve the security, performance, and scalability of network management systems. By isolating SNMP traffic, applying strict access controls, and utilizing encryption, organizations can protect their network infrastructure from unauthorized access, interception, and tampering. Network segmentation also enhances the efficiency of SNMP-based monitoring systems by reducing congestion and ensuring that network management traffic is handled separately from regular data traffic. As organizations continue to scale and adopt more complex network architectures, leveraging SNMP within a segmented network becomes an essential best practice to ensure secure, reliable, and effective network management.

SNMP in Compliance and Auditing

As organizations face increasing regulatory pressure to secure their networks and protect sensitive data, ensuring that network management practices align with compliance standards has become a top priority. SNMP, or Simple Network Management Protocol, is a widely used protocol for monitoring and managing network devices. While SNMP provides valuable insight into network performance and health, it also introduces potential security risks if not properly configured or monitored. In industries where compliance with standards such as HIPAA, PCI DSS, or SOX is required, organizations must implement robust auditing and security controls over SNMP to meet regulatory requirements.

One of the fundamental aspects of compliance is ensuring the integrity and confidentiality of data, especially when it comes to network management systems that monitor and control critical infrastructure. SNMP has traditionally been viewed as a protocol that lacks sufficient security mechanisms, particularly in older versions like SNMPv1 and SNMPv2c. These versions transmit community strings and management data in plaintext, making it vulnerable to interception and unauthorized access. For compliance with modern security standards, SNMPv1 and SNMPv2c are often deemed inadequate for managing network devices in sensitive or regulated environments. The adoption of SNMPv3 is a key step in securing SNMP communications, as it offers improved security features such as authentication, encryption, and message integrity.

In compliance-driven environments, using SNMPv3 is essential, as it addresses many of the security concerns inherent in earlier versions. SNMPv3 allows for strong authentication through hash-based algorithms like HMAC-SHA or HMAC-MD5, ensuring that only authorized users or systems can access SNMP data. Additionally, SNMPv3 supports encryption, which ensures that sensitive network management data is protected from unauthorized access during transmission. By enabling both authentication and encryption, organizations can meet data protection requirements laid out by various compliance standards, making SNMPv3 a cornerstone of secure network management in regulated environments.

Beyond the security features of SNMPv3, another critical aspect of using SNMP in compliance and auditing is the ability to track and log all SNMP-related activities. Compliance frameworks often require organizations to maintain detailed records of network activity, including who accessed or modified specific devices and what changes were made. SNMP managers, when configured correctly, can provide comprehensive logs that capture all SNMP queries, modifications, and responses. These logs are crucial for auditing purposes and can be used to detect unauthorized access, misconfigurations, or unusual activity that could signal a breach or an attempted attack.

Regular auditing of SNMP configurations and activities is vital for maintaining compliance with regulatory standards. In many cases, auditing and logging requirements go beyond just ensuring that SNMP traffic is secure. Regulatory frameworks often mandate that organizations demonstrate how they have controlled access to sensitive systems and that they are able to prove who made changes to critical infrastructure. SNMP logs and access records provide the necessary evidence for audits, showing that only authorized personnel have had the ability to perform read or write operations on SNMP-enabled devices. These logs can be stored centrally and analyzed for suspicious behavior, ensuring that the organization can both prevent and respond to potential compliance violations.

The principle of least privilege is a key tenet in many compliance frameworks, and SNMP access control mechanisms must align with this principle. By configuring SNMP with proper role-based access control (RBAC), organizations can ensure that only authorized users are allowed to access or modify specific MIB objects based on their roles within the organization. For example, network operators may be given read-only access to device statistics, while network engineers are granted read-write access to make necessary configurations. This minimizes the risk of unauthorized or accidental changes to network devices, which is critical in maintaining compliance with standards such as SOX (Sarbanes-Oxley) and PCI DSS (Payment Card Industry Data Security Standard).

Compliance standards often require detailed documentation of network management practices, including how devices are monitored, who has access to SNMP, and how SNMP data is secured. Organizations need to maintain an up-to-date inventory of all SNMP-enabled devices, document who has access to SNMP data, and ensure that security policies are enforced consistently across the network. By leveraging SNMPv3's security features and maintaining robust access controls, organizations can demonstrate that they are following industry best practices for network security and adhering to compliance guidelines. Proper documentation of SNMP configurations and security settings provides clear evidence of compliance and strengthens the organization's position during audits.

The ability to generate SNMP traps for important network events also plays a role in compliance and auditing. SNMP traps are notifications sent by network devices to alert administrators about events such as device failures, configuration changes, or security incidents. These traps are crucial for real-time monitoring and incident response, but they also contribute to compliance efforts by providing a historical record of critical events. By collecting SNMP traps in a centralized logging system, organizations can ensure that any security incidents or operational issues are logged and can be reviewed during audits. These logs can serve as evidence that appropriate actions were taken in response to incidents and that the organization is monitoring its devices in accordance with regulatory requirements.

In addition to internal logging and auditing, SNMP can be integrated with centralized security information and event management (SIEM) systems. SIEM platforms aggregate logs and provide real-time analysis of security data, which helps identify potential threats, vulnerabilities, or compliance violations. By forwarding SNMP logs and traps to a SIEM system, organizations can gain a broader view of network activity, correlate SNMP-related events with other security data, and generate alerts for unusual or suspicious behavior. This integration helps organizations respond to threats more quickly and effectively, ensuring that they remain compliant with security standards while reducing the likelihood of security incidents.

Network segmentation is another important strategy for ensuring that SNMP is used in a compliant manner. By isolating SNMP traffic on dedicated management networks or VLANs, organizations can prevent unauthorized access to SNMP data from general users or external attackers. This is particularly important in environments where sensitive information is being monitored or managed. Compliance frameworks often require that management traffic be isolated from user traffic to reduce the risk of exposure or tampering. Network segmentation ensures that SNMP traffic is confined to trusted networks, making it harder for attackers to intercept or manipulate SNMP communications.

Regular vulnerability assessments and penetration testing are also vital components of SNMP-related compliance. Security experts should periodically test SNMP configurations to identify potential weaknesses or misconfigurations that could lead to compliance violations or security breaches. Vulnerability assessments help ensure that SNMP implementations are secure and aligned with current security policies and industry standards.

In the context of compliance and auditing, SNMP serves as both a monitoring tool and a potential security risk if not properly configured. By adopting SNMPv3, enforcing strict access controls, logging SNMP activity, and implementing network segmentation, organizations can meet compliance requirements while reducing the risks associated with network management. Regular audits, combined with a proactive approach to SNMP security, ensure that network management systems remain secure, efficient, and aligned with regulatory standards.

SNMP and VPN Monitoring

As organizations continue to adopt more complex network architectures to support distributed workforces and cloud-based services, the need for robust monitoring solutions becomes increasingly important. One of the most widely used tools for managing network devices is SNMP (Simple Network Management Protocol), which allows administrators to monitor the status, health, and performance of devices on the network. When combined with

VPNs (Virtual Private Networks), SNMP plays a critical role in ensuring secure, reliable, and efficient VPN operations by providing visibility into the health of VPN connections, performance metrics, and network traffic. VPNs have become a staple of remote work and secure communications, but without proper monitoring, organizations risk exposing themselves to vulnerabilities that could be exploited by malicious actors.

VPNs enable secure communication over public or untrusted networks by encrypting data traffic between clients and network resources. The adoption of VPN technologies has grown rapidly in response to the increasing demand for secure remote access to corporate networks, especially in the context of a more decentralized workforce. However, VPNs introduce unique challenges when it comes to monitoring and performance management. As VPN connections serve as gateways to critical internal resources, maintaining their performance, availability, and security is vital for ensuring business continuity and safeguarding sensitive data.

SNMP provides a reliable method for monitoring VPN devices, including VPN gateways, firewalls, and routers. These devices act as endpoints for establishing and managing VPN connections, handling tasks such as encryption, decryption, traffic routing, and authentication. Through SNMP, administrators can collect performance data from these devices, including bandwidth usage, connection status, error rates, and resource utilization, all of which are essential for understanding the health and performance of VPN connections. By querying SNMP-enabled devices, administrators can obtain critical insights into how well VPN connections are functioning and whether there are any issues that need immediate attention.

One of the key aspects of SNMP in VPN monitoring is its ability to track bandwidth usage. VPNs often experience heavy traffic due to the encryption and decryption of data, which can introduce latency and consume significant network resources. SNMP can be used to monitor the traffic passing through VPN gateways, providing administrators with real-time visibility into the amount of data being transmitted across the VPN. This allows administrators to identify potential bottlenecks or performance degradation, enabling them to take corrective action, such as optimizing the routing configuration, adjusting VPN parameters, or increasing available bandwidth. By continuously monitoring bandwidth usage through SNMP, organizations can ensure that their VPN infrastructure can handle the demands of remote users and critical applications.

In addition to bandwidth monitoring, SNMP is useful for tracking VPN tunnel status and health. VPNs rely on various protocols, such as IPsec, SSL, or MPLS, to establish secure communication channels. By using SNMP to monitor the status of VPN tunnels, administrators can quickly identify whether tunnels are up or down and take action if a connection is lost or experiencing high levels of packet loss or latency. Monitoring the status of VPN tunnels ensures that users can access network resources securely and reliably, minimizing downtime and improving overall service quality. SNMP also allows administrators to detect configuration changes that may affect VPN performance, such as changes to IP address assignments, authentication settings, or encryption algorithms.

The ability to monitor VPN error rates through SNMP is another valuable tool for troubleshooting and maintaining VPN performance. VPN connections are susceptible to various types of errors, including authentication failures, encryption mismatches, and routing issues. SNMP can capture these errors, allowing administrators to identify the root cause of VPN issues more quickly. For example, high error rates may indicate that VPN clients are using incompatible encryption settings or that there is a misconfiguration in the VPN gateway. By using SNMP to gather error data, administrators can address issues proactively, minimizing the impact on users and improving the overall stability and reliability of the VPN infrastructure.

Another key benefit of SNMP in VPN monitoring is its ability to integrate with centralized network management platforms. These platforms can aggregate SNMP data from multiple VPN devices, providing a unified view of the VPN infrastructure's health and performance. By consolidating data from VPN gateways, firewalls, routers, and other network devices, administrators can gain a comprehensive understanding of the VPN environment and identify trends, anomalies, and potential issues. SNMP-enabled network management systems can generate reports, dashboards, and alerts, helping administrators monitor VPN performance in real-time and respond quickly to incidents. This integration streamlines VPN monitoring, making it easier for network administrators to manage VPN infrastructure at scale.

VPN security is another area where SNMP plays a crucial role. VPNs provide encrypted access to sensitive data, and as such, they must be closely monitored to ensure that they are not vulnerable to attacks. SNMP can be used to track security-related events on VPN devices, such as failed authentication attempts, unusual traffic patterns, or suspicious login activity. This data can be forwarded to a centralized security information and event management (SIEM) system for further analysis and correlation with other security logs. By using SNMP to monitor VPN security events, organizations can detect potential threats and take action before they escalate into more serious security incidents.

Additionally, SNMP can help track the performance of the underlying infrastructure supporting the VPN, such as the physical and virtual servers, routers, and network appliances. VPNs depend on a variety of network devices to establish and maintain secure connections, and any issues with these devices can affect VPN performance. SNMP allows administrators to monitor the health and status of these devices, ensuring that they are functioning optimally and not introducing additional latency or bottlenecks to VPN traffic. For instance, monitoring CPU utilization and memory usage on VPN gateway devices can help identify performance degradation that could impact the overall VPN experience for users.

In a large-scale enterprise network with numerous remote users, SNMP is essential for ensuring that VPN infrastructure can scale to meet growing demands. As the number of remote users and VPN connections increases, the performance and reliability of VPN services can be impacted. SNMP provides a way to monitor how well the infrastructure is handling this growth, enabling administrators to make informed decisions about resource allocation, hardware upgrades, and network optimizations. By continually monitoring VPN performance through SNMP, organizations can ensure that their VPN services remain responsive and reliable even as user demand increases.

Effective VPN monitoring using SNMP also contributes to regulatory compliance and security best practices. Many compliance standards, such as PCI DSS, HIPAA, and GDPR, require organizations to secure remote access to sensitive data. By using SNMP to monitor VPN performance, encryption standards, and user activity, organizations can demonstrate that they are meeting compliance requirements related to secure communications. SNMP can help track encryption levels, monitor unauthorized access attempts, and ensure that VPN systems are configured according to industry standards, providing a valuable layer of oversight for compliance and auditing purposes.

In modern network management, VPNs are integral to secure communications, and SNMP is an indispensable tool for monitoring these networks. With its ability to provide insights into bandwidth usage, tunnel health, error rates, security events, and overall infrastructure performance, SNMP helps ensure that VPNs operate efficiently, securely, and reliably. By integrating SNMP into the VPN monitoring framework, organizations can proactively manage and optimize their VPN infrastructure, ensuring that remote users have secure, uninterrupted access to critical resources.

SNMP in Industrial Control Systems

Industrial Control Systems (ICS) are used to manage and automate the operations of critical infrastructure such as power plants, water treatment facilities, manufacturing lines, and transportation systems. These systems are composed of various components such as Supervisory Control and Data Acquisition (SCADA) systems, Programmable Logic Controllers (PLCs), remote terminal units (RTUs), sensors, and actuators, all of which require robust monitoring and management to ensure smooth and efficient operation. SNMP, traditionally used in enterprise IT environments, has found its place in the world of industrial control due to its ability to monitor networked devices and systems efficiently. When implemented correctly, SNMP plays a vital role in enhancing the visibility, performance, and security of ICS.

The use of SNMP in industrial control systems offers a way to remotely monitor and manage the diverse array of devices that make up the infrastructure. Industrial environments are often highly distributed, with devices spread across large physical areas or even multiple geographic locations. In such settings, SNMP provides a standardized protocol for communication, enabling centralized monitoring and management of devices that might otherwise be difficult to access directly. Devices like PLCs, sensors, and RTUs that are part of an industrial process can expose important operational data through SNMP, allowing administrators to assess the health of equipment, track system performance, and detect potential issues before they escalate into more significant failures.

One of the primary benefits of SNMP in ICS is its ability to gather real-time data from networked devices. Devices like PLCs, which control machines and automated processes, can send SNMP traps or respond to SNMP queries with performance metrics such as processing power, memory utilization, and operational status. This data helps administrators track the state of industrial equipment, ensuring that critical processes continue to run without interruptions. For instance, monitoring the temperature of motors, pressure in valves, or current flowing through circuit breakers can provide early warnings of potential faults or failures. SNMP can also monitor communication between different components of the system, helping identify network issues that may affect the flow of data or the performance of operations.

In addition to real-time monitoring, SNMP in ICS enables the collection of historical data that can be analyzed to identify trends and optimize system performance. The ability to collect and store data over time allows administrators to detect inefficiencies in the system, such as equipment operating at suboptimal levels or excessive energy consumption. This data is valuable not only for improving the performance of the industrial control system but also for planning future upgrades or replacements of aging equipment. Furthermore, SNMP can be used to track device availability, ensuring that all components of the ICS are online and functioning as expected.

Another important aspect of using SNMP in industrial control systems is the ability to integrate it with other monitoring and control systems. In many industrial environments, SCADA systems serve as the central hub for managing and controlling industrial processes. SCADA systems can use SNMP to gather data from various devices, including PLCs, sensors, and RTUs, and present that data on centralized dashboards. The integration of SNMP into SCADA systems allows operators to monitor the health of all connected devices in real time, providing a comprehensive view of the entire industrial operation. In addition, SNMP can be used to trigger alarms and notifications when certain thresholds are exceeded, alerting operators to take corrective action.

However, the use of SNMP in ICS is not without its challenges, particularly when it comes to security. Industrial control systems are critical to the functioning of society's most essential infrastructure, making them an attractive target for cyberattacks. In the past, many ICS environments relied on legacy systems that used older versions of SNMP (such as SNMPv1 or SNMPv2c), which are inherently insecure. These versions transmit data, including community strings, in plaintext, leaving them vulnerable to interception, unauthorized access, and manipulation. Given the critical nature of ICS, using insecure versions of SNMP poses a significant risk.

To mitigate these risks, organizations must adopt SNMPv3, which offers improved security features, including message authentication, encryption, and message integrity. SNMPv3 allows administrators to configure strong user-based authentication, ensuring that only authorized users can access or modify SNMP data. Additionally, SNMPv3 encrypts communication, protecting sensitive operational data from being intercepted. By implementing SNMPv3 in ICS, organizations can enhance the security of their networked devices and ensure that SNMP-based communication is secure from both internal and external threats.

Access control is another essential aspect of securing SNMP in industrial control systems. To reduce the risk of unauthorized access, organizations should implement strict access control policies, ensuring that only trusted users and systems are allowed to interact with SNMP-enabled devices. This can be achieved through the use of network segmentation and firewalls, which restrict access to SNMP traffic to specific management systems or IP addresses. By isolating SNMP traffic from general network traffic, organizations can reduce the risk of cyberattacks exploiting vulnerable SNMP implementations.

The integration of SNMP with Industrial Internet of Things (IIoT) devices further extends the role of SNMP in ICS. IIoT devices, such as smart sensors and connected industrial machines, are increasingly becoming part of modern industrial networks. These devices rely on SNMP for monitoring and managing their performance, providing valuable data to improve operational efficiency. By enabling SNMP communication between IIoT devices and central monitoring systems, organizations can gain real-time insights into the condition of individual components and systems, allowing for predictive maintenance and reduced downtime. This integration plays a key role in optimizing the overall efficiency of industrial control systems and reducing operational costs.

While SNMP is a powerful tool for monitoring and managing industrial control systems, organizations must carefully configure and maintain their SNMP implementation to ensure its effectiveness. Regularly updating SNMP agents, implementing strong authentication protocols, and performing routine security audits are essential practices to ensure that SNMP continues to provide accurate and secure monitoring in ICS environments. Furthermore, organizations should consider integrating SNMP monitoring with other security and monitoring tools, such as intrusion detection systems (IDS), to enhance their overall network security posture.

In conclusion, SNMP plays a vital role in ensuring the efficiency, performance, and security of industrial control systems. By enabling real-time monitoring of devices and systems, collecting performance data, and integrating with SCADA systems and IIoT devices, SNMP provides valuable insights into the operational health of critical infrastructure. However, to maximize the benefits of SNMP and minimize security risks, organizations must adopt SNMPv3, implement strong access control measures, and regularly monitor and maintain their SNMP systems. Through careful planning and implementation, SNMP can significantly improve the reliability and security of industrial control systems, ensuring the continued smooth operation of vital services and infrastructure.

SNMP in Industrial Control Systems

Industrial Control Systems (ICS) are an integral part of critical infrastructure across industries such as manufacturing, energy, water treatment, and transportation. These systems manage and control industrial processes, often consisting of large-scale machinery and automated systems that require continuous monitoring to ensure optimal performance and avoid potential failures. SNMP, or Simple Network Management Protocol, plays a crucial role in the monitoring, management, and optimization of devices within ICS environments. SNMP allows administrators to collect vital performance data from networked devices, providing them with real-time insight into the operational health of an entire system. However, the use of SNMP in these environments comes with unique challenges due to the mission-critical nature of the infrastructure and the potential vulnerabilities of legacy systems.

The role of SNMP in ICS environments is to provide a standardized method for monitoring a wide range of devices, from programmable logic controllers (PLCs) and remote terminal units (RTUs) to sensors and human-machine interfaces (HMIs). These devices collect and transmit data that is crucial for running industrial processes effectively. In environments where physical assets are scattered across vast areas or in remote locations, SNMP enables administrators to gather real-time information from these devices without the need for physical intervention. The protocol provides a way to remotely monitor system health, including metrics like memory usage, CPU load, network traffic, device status, and error rates, which are all essential for maintaining uninterrupted operations.

SNMP facilitates the monitoring of these devices by allowing administrators to query specific attributes exposed by SNMP agents embedded in the devices. These attributes can include environmental conditions like temperature, pressure, or humidity, as well as the status of critical components like motors, pumps, and valves. Through regular SNMP queries, administrators can track the real-time performance of these devices and identify potential issues before they escalate into costly or catastrophic failures. For example, monitoring the temperature of industrial machines can help identify overheating before it leads to permanent damage, allowing for timely intervention to prevent costly repairs or system downtime.

In addition to real-time monitoring, SNMP also enables the collection of historical data that can be used for performance analysis and optimization. By analyzing trends in system performance, administrators can identify areas for improvement, such as inefficient processes or underperforming equipment. This historical data also aids in capacity planning and resource allocation, as administrators can predict when certain devices or processes may need to be upgraded or replaced to meet future demands. This predictive ability is crucial for ensuring that ICS environments run smoothly without unexpected disruptions.

One of the most significant advantages of using SNMP in ICS environments is its ability to provide a centralized view of the system. In large-scale industrial operations, devices may be located across a vast geographic area, making it difficult to monitor individual systems directly. By integrating SNMP with a centralized management platform, administrators can gain a comprehensive overview of the entire infrastructure. These platforms can aggregate SNMP data from various devices, offering a unified interface where performance data is displayed, analyzed, and acted upon. This centralized approach streamlines monitoring efforts and allows administrators to respond quickly to any potential issues.

However, SNMP's widespread use in ICS environments also introduces several security concerns. Many ICS devices were not originally designed with security in mind, especially older devices that still rely on SNMPv1 or SNMPv2c. These versions of the protocol transmit data, including community strings, in plaintext, which makes it relatively easy for attackers to intercept and exploit sensitive information. In the context of industrial systems, where unauthorized access could have devastating consequences, these security weaknesses are particularly problematic. As a result, many experts recommend upgrading to SNMPv3, which offers enhanced security features, such as encryption and message integrity, to protect the data being exchanged between devices and monitoring systems.

In addition to upgrading to SNMPv3, organizations must also implement robust access control mechanisms to limit who can interact with SNMP-enabled devices. Access to industrial systems should be restricted to authorized personnel and systems to prevent unauthorized monitoring or manipulation of critical infrastructure. This can be accomplished through the use of firewalls, access control lists (ACLs), and network segmentation to ensure that only trusted devices are allowed to send or receive SNMP traffic. Further, SNMP traps, which notify administrators of specific events such as device failures or threshold breaches, should be configured to send alerts only to trusted systems to prevent attackers from spoofing or intercepting these messages.

Another security measure to consider when using SNMP in ICS is the monitoring of SNMP activity. Regularly reviewing SNMP logs and alerts can help administrators identify unusual patterns or potential security breaches. For example, if an SNMP manager is repeatedly attempting to access devices it should not have access to, this could be an indication of an attempted attack or an internal security issue. Likewise, reviewing SNMP traps and logs can help identify any devices that are consistently reporting errors or experiencing performance issues, allowing administrators to address these problems before they lead to system downtime or failure.

The integration of SNMP with other monitoring systems, such as SCADA (Supervisory Control and Data Acquisition) platforms, further enhances its effectiveness in ICS. SCADA systems are commonly used to control and monitor industrial processes, and integrating SNMP into these platforms allows administrators to monitor networked devices alongside the industrial equipment they manage. For example, a SCADA system might be used to monitor the status of pumps, motors, and valves, while SNMP can provide additional information about the health of the PLCs or RTUs controlling these devices. By combining data from both systems, administrators gain a more complete picture of the state of the entire infrastructure, making it easier to identify potential issues and take corrective action.

One of the challenges associated with SNMP in ICS is the lack of standardization across devices. Industrial environments often rely on a wide variety of manufacturers and equipment, which may implement

SNMP in slightly different ways. This can make it difficult to collect consistent data or integrate devices from different vendors into a unified monitoring platform. To address this challenge, many organizations develop custom SNMP MIBs (Management Information Bases) to define how SNMP should interact with specific devices, ensuring consistency in the way data is collected and monitored across the system. These custom MIBs can be tailored to the unique requirements of the industrial environment, providing a standardized method for collecting and analyzing performance data from a variety of devices.

Incorporating SNMP into an industrial control system enhances visibility, improves operational efficiency, and reduces downtime by enabling real-time monitoring of critical devices. However, it is essential to recognize the security risks and challenges associated with SNMP, particularly in legacy systems that may not have been designed with modern cybersecurity in mind. By adopting SNMPv3, implementing strict access control measures, and integrating SNMP with other monitoring systems, organizations can effectively mitigate these risks and ensure the safe and efficient operation of their industrial control systems.

SNMP Tools and Utilities

SNMP (Simple Network Management Protocol) is an essential protocol used to monitor and manage networked devices. Through its ability to gather performance metrics and detect faults in devices such as routers, switches, servers, and firewalls, SNMP has become a critical tool for network administrators. The sheer complexity of modern networks requires robust SNMP tools and utilities that help administrators efficiently manage these networks, diagnose problems, and ensure the infrastructure runs smoothly. These tools range from command-line utilities to full-fledged graphical network management platforms, and each tool provides specific features suited to different monitoring needs and environments.

One of the most commonly used SNMP tools is the SNMPwalk command-line utility. SNMPwalk allows users to query an SNMP-enabled device to retrieve an entire set of data from its Management Information Base (MIB). This tool is typically used to explore all the available SNMP data exposed by a device. For example, when an SNMP manager runs an SNMPwalk on a network device, it can receive all the MIB objects related to that device, including information about its network interfaces, CPU utilization, memory status, and much more. The ability to query a device and receive a full list of objects makes SNMPwalk a powerful tool for network discovery and troubleshooting.

Alongside SNMPwalk, there are other utilities such as SNMPget and SNMPset, which are used to interact with SNMP-enabled devices in more specific ways. SNMPget is used to query individual data points from a device, requesting the value of a specific MIB object. This can be particularly useful when administrators want to check the status of a single parameter, such as the bandwidth usage on a specific network interface. On the other hand, SNMPset allows users to modify the values of MIB objects on a device. For example, an administrator can change the configuration of a device using SNMPset, such as enabling or disabling network interfaces, updating system settings, or adjusting thresholds for certain metrics.

Beyond the basic command-line tools, there are several more sophisticated SNMP utilities designed to provide graphical interfaces for easier management of SNMP devices. Network monitoring software such as PRTG Network Monitor, SolarWinds Network Performance Monitor, and Nagios provide comprehensive SNMP-based monitoring solutions. These tools come with built-in support for SNMPv1, SNMPv2c, and SNMPv3, and they can automatically discover SNMP devices on the network. Once devices are discovered, the software presents data collected from SNMP agents in real time, displaying performance metrics in easy-to-read graphs, dashboards, and reports. These tools often include alerting features, which can notify administrators when a device exceeds predefined thresholds for metrics like CPU usage, disk space, or network traffic. Alerts are typically sent through email, SMS, or integration with other IT management systems, ensuring that network issues are detected and addressed promptly.

In addition to these commercial solutions, there are open-source alternatives such as Cacti, Zabbix, and Observium. These platforms offer similar functionality, including SNMP polling, alerting, and graphing. Cacti, for example, is a popular open-source tool known for its powerful graphing capabilities, allowing administrators to visualize a wide range of metrics from SNMP-enabled devices. Zabbix, another open-source monitoring solution, offers comprehensive network and application monitoring with support for SNMP and other protocols. It includes advanced features such as automated configuration, event correlation, and a web-based user interface. These open-source tools are favored by many organizations due to their flexibility, scalability, and the absence of licensing fees, although they may require more customization and manual setup compared to commercial solutions.

For security-conscious administrators, tools that specialize in SNMP security auditing and vulnerability scanning are available. These tools help administrators assess the security posture of SNMP implementations across their network. A common problem with SNMP is the use of default community strings, such as "public" and "private," which are widely known and often remain unchanged. These tools can scan for devices using these weak community strings and help identify devices that may be at risk. Some tools also check for SNMPv1 or SNMPv2c usage, which lack adequate security features like encryption and authentication. By identifying these vulnerabilities, administrators can take corrective actions, such as upgrading to SNMPv3 and changing community strings to improve the security of their network devices.

In addition to standalone tools, SNMP is also integrated into various IT service management (ITSM) and system monitoring platforms. These platforms typically use SNMP to collect data on network devices, systems, and applications, allowing IT teams to manage performance, incidents, and changes through a unified interface. These solutions integrate SNMP monitoring with ticketing systems, allowing administrators to automatically generate service tickets in response to SNMP traps or alerts. These integrations help streamline incident management processes and improve overall response times.

SNMP's role in managing industrial control systems (ICS) also requires specialized tools and utilities. In ICS environments, devices like programmable logic controllers (PLCs) and supervisory control and data acquisition (SCADA) systems often use SNMP for monitoring and control. These environments require real-time monitoring, high availability, and tight security. SNMP-based tools used in industrial environments must be capable of handling the specific needs of these systems, including high-volume data collection, extended device support, and integration with other ICS management protocols. Tools in this space are often custom-built or tailored for specific industrial applications, providing a level of control and monitoring that goes beyond traditional enterprise IT networks.

In addition to monitoring tools, SNMP utilities are used to troubleshoot and test SNMP communications. SNMP Tester, for example, is a utility that can be used to verify whether SNMP agents are responding properly and to test specific SNMP requests. This tool can help diagnose connectivity issues, check the response times of SNMP devices, and verify whether SNMP community strings are functioning correctly. SNMP Tester is particularly useful when deploying new SNMP devices or after changes have been made to the network. It helps ensure that SNMP communication is working as expected and that devices are correctly configured to respond to SNMP queries.

Another critical aspect of SNMP toolsets is the ability to configure SNMP agents on network devices. Many SNMP tools allow administrators to set configuration parameters remotely, including the community strings, the SNMP version in use, and the devices' MIB settings. This remote configuration capability is vital for managing large-scale networks where manually configuring SNMP settings on each device would be time-consuming and error-prone. By using centralized tools for SNMP agent configuration, administrators can streamline the deployment and management of SNMP across a wide array of devices.

SNMP tools and utilities play a crucial role in the ongoing management, security, and optimization of networked systems. From simple command-line utilities like SNMPwalk and SNMPget to complex network monitoring platforms like SolarWinds and Zabbix, these tools offer administrators the capability to gather critical data, diagnose issues, and ensure the health of their network infrastructure. With the growing importance of SNMP in modern network management, having the right set of tools is essential for administrators to maintain an efficient, secure, and reliable network. Whether for troubleshooting, performance monitoring, or security auditing, SNMP tools provide the necessary features to manage large-scale networks effectively.

Open-Source SNMP Management Platforms

Open-source SNMP management platforms have become an essential tool for network administrators who seek to monitor, manage, and optimize their networks without the constraints of proprietary software. These platforms provide an accessible, customizable, and cost-effective solution for SNMP-based monitoring and management. As more organizations recognize the benefits of open-source software, they increasingly rely on these platforms to collect real-time data from SNMP-enabled devices, detect network issues, and ensure the health and performance of their infrastructure. By offering flexibility, community support, and scalability, open-source SNMP management platforms are helping administrators gain greater control over their network environments while reducing the cost of ownership associated with commercial alternatives.

One of the most significant advantages of open-source SNMP management platforms is their flexibility. These platforms can be tailored to meet the specific needs of an organization, allowing administrators to add custom features, integrate third-party tools, or adjust the platform's capabilities to match their unique network architecture. For instance, open-source platforms typically offer the ability to modify the underlying code, enabling organizations to build custom plugins or dashboards that display SNMP data in the format most useful for their operations. This level of customization is especially valuable in complex or specialized environments where off-the-shelf solutions may fall short.

Another key benefit of open-source SNMP management platforms is the cost savings. Proprietary SNMP management software often requires expensive licensing fees, ongoing maintenance costs, and vendor-specific support contracts. In contrast, open-source platforms are free to use, which makes them highly attractive to organizations operating with limited budgets. Furthermore, because these platforms are community-driven, organizations benefit from a wide range of updates, patches, and new features released by the community, often at no cost. This not only reduces upfront expenses but also ensures that the platform remains up-to-date and relevant as new network devices and SNMP versions emerge.

Several popular open-source SNMP management platforms have gained traction among network administrators due to their comprehensive features and ease of use. One of the most well-known is Cacti, a network monitoring platform that uses SNMP to gather data from network devices and generate detailed graphs and reports. Cacti's primary strength lies in its powerful graphing engine, which enables administrators to visualize a wide range of network performance metrics, such as bandwidth usage, CPU load, and memory utilization. By using SNMP to collect data from devices like routers, switches, and servers, Cacti helps administrators track historical trends, identify potential bottlenecks, and optimize their network infrastructure. Additionally, Cacti supports a wide variety of plugins, making it highly customizable for different network environments.

Another popular open-source SNMP management platform is Zabbix. Zabbix is a comprehensive monitoring solution that supports SNMP and a wide array of other protocols, making it a versatile choice for network administrators. It provides a centralized platform for monitoring the performance of SNMP-enabled devices, servers, applications, and services. Zabbix's strength lies in its ability to perform both proactive and reactive monitoring. Administrators can configure the platform to generate alerts when certain thresholds are exceeded, such as high CPU utilization or network downtime. Zabbix also includes advanced features such as real-time monitoring, reporting, and trending, all of which help administrators maintain the health of their infrastructure. Its scalability is another attractive feature, as it can easily handle large networks with thousands of devices.

Observium is another noteworthy open-source platform that provides SNMP-based network monitoring. Observium focuses on simplicity and ease of use, making it ideal for organizations that require a straightforward, intuitive interface for monitoring their devices. Like other open-source SNMP platforms, Observium collects data from

SNMP-enabled devices and displays the information in a user-friendly web interface. The platform includes features such as automatic device discovery, which helps streamline the setup process, and customizable graphs and dashboards for tracking device performance. Observium also supports SNMPv3, offering enhanced security features like encryption and authentication, making it suitable for modern network environments that require robust security measures.

Nagios, a widely recognized open-source network monitoring system, also offers SNMP support through plugins and extensions. Nagios is known for its flexibility and extensibility, enabling administrators to customize the platform to fit their specific network monitoring needs. With Nagios, network administrators can monitor SNMP-enabled devices, servers, and applications, receiving alerts when issues arise or when thresholds are exceeded. Nagios also integrates with other open-source tools and monitoring platforms, enabling administrators to build a comprehensive monitoring solution that spans various parts of their infrastructure.

One of the key features that many open-source SNMP management platforms share is their ability to provide real-time monitoring and alerting. These platforms can track SNMP data from devices and trigger notifications when critical thresholds are reached, such as when a device goes offline, a network link becomes congested, or when CPU or memory usage exceeds a specified limit. The ability to set up these real-time alerts is essential for network administrators, as it enables them to respond to issues quickly, often before they escalate into more significant problems. Additionally, many open-source SNMP platforms allow users to define custom alerts based on the specific needs of their network, ensuring that only the most relevant issues are flagged for attention.

In addition to real-time monitoring and alerting, many open-source SNMP management platforms offer detailed reporting and visualization features. These platforms often include the ability to generate graphs, charts, and reports that display network performance over time. By analyzing historical data, administrators can identify trends and make informed decisions about network optimization and resource allocation. Some platforms also allow users to create custom dashboards, which provide at-a-glance visibility into the health of various devices and systems across the network. The ability to visualize performance metrics in an easily interpretable format is invaluable for making data-driven decisions about network management.

For organizations that require a high level of control and customization, the open-source nature of these platforms is a significant advantage. Open-source SNMP management platforms allow network administrators to modify the software to meet the unique needs of their infrastructure, whether through custom plugins, scripting, or integration with other systems. This level of flexibility is particularly beneficial in large or complex network environments where off-the-shelf solutions may not provide the necessary functionality.

Open-source SNMP management platforms also benefit from strong community support. As these platforms are developed and maintained by a global community of developers and users, administrators can rely on a wealth of knowledge and resources when implementing or troubleshooting their monitoring solution. Forums, documentation, and user-contributed plugins further enhance the value of these platforms, making it easier for administrators to customize and optimize their setup. Additionally, because these platforms are open source, they tend to evolve rapidly, with new features and improvements being added regularly by the community.

While open-source SNMP management platforms offer a wide range of features and benefits, they also come with certain challenges. These platforms often require more technical expertise to set up and configure compared to commercial alternatives. Administrators must be comfortable with installation processes, configuration files, and sometimes even code modifications. Additionally, while the community provides valuable support, the lack of official customer service or guaranteed updates can be a drawback for some organizations. However, for those with the expertise and resources to manage and customize the tools, open-source SNMP management platforms offer a cost-effective and flexible solution for monitoring and managing networked devices.

In modern IT environments, where scalability, flexibility, and cost-effectiveness are increasingly important, open-source SNMP management platforms provide organizations with the tools they need to monitor their network infrastructure effectively. From monitoring network performance and resource usage to ensuring uptime and security, these platforms offer a powerful alternative to proprietary solutions. Whether it is through real-time monitoring, customizable reporting, or advanced alerting, open-source SNMP management platforms empower network administrators to keep their networks running smoothly while maintaining control over the tools they use.

Commercial SNMP Monitoring Solutions

In today's rapidly evolving digital landscape, where network infrastructure supports critical business operations, the need for effective network monitoring solutions is more important than ever. SNMP (Simple Network Management Protocol) is one of the most widely used protocols for monitoring and managing network devices, including routers, switches, servers, and other hardware. While open-source SNMP monitoring tools offer flexibility and customization, many organizations opt for commercial SNMP monitoring solutions due to their robust feature sets, scalability, and dedicated support. Commercial solutions offer more than just monitoring; they provide comprehensive, integrated platforms designed to optimize performance, troubleshoot issues, ensure security, and maintain the reliability of enterprise networks.

One of the main advantages of commercial SNMP monitoring solutions is the comprehensive support and resources they offer. These solutions often come with a dedicated customer support team that can assist organizations with setup, configuration, troubleshooting, and optimization. For large enterprises, having access to professional support can save valuable time and ensure that the monitoring system is set up correctly, minimizing the risk of misconfigurations that could impact network performance. Additionally, commercial vendors typically offer training, documentation, and user resources to help administrators get the most out of the platform. This level of support and assistance can be invaluable, particularly for organizations with limited in-house expertise or resources for managing complex network environments.

Scalability is another key factor that drives organizations to adopt commercial SNMP monitoring solutions. Many commercial platforms are designed to scale with the needs of an organization, making them suitable for networks of all sizes, from small businesses to large enterprises. As a network grows, so too does the need for monitoring and managing an increasing number of devices. Commercial solutions provide the flexibility to expand the monitoring system as needed, whether by adding more devices, users, or regions. These platforms are built to handle the complexities of large-scale networks, offering features like distributed monitoring, multi-user access, and real-time performance analysis for thousands of devices across various geographical locations.

In addition to scalability, commercial SNMP monitoring solutions often come with advanced features for network performance optimization and troubleshooting. These platforms are designed to help administrators quickly identify and resolve network issues, reducing downtime and improving overall network efficiency. Features such as advanced alerting, automated reporting, and detailed dashboards allow administrators to monitor critical metrics in real time and receive immediate notifications if something goes wrong. For example, if a device goes offline or a network link experiences heavy congestion, the monitoring solution can send an alert to the administrator, enabling a fast response to mitigate the issue. Commercial tools may also include root cause analysis capabilities, helping administrators drill down into the data to identify the underlying causes of network problems, such as faulty hardware, misconfigurations, or insufficient bandwidth.

Security is another area where commercial SNMP monitoring solutions excel. With the growing number of cyberattacks and the increasing sophistication of malicious actors, ensuring the security of SNMP communications is paramount. Commercial solutions often support SNMPv3, which provides stronger security features than earlier versions of SNMP. SNMPv3 includes message authentication, encryption, and data integrity, ensuring that sensitive network data remains protected from unauthorized access and tampering. Commercial SNMP monitoring solutions may also include advanced security monitoring features, such as anomaly detection, intrusion prevention, and the ability to integrate with other security tools like

SIEM (Security Information and Event Management) systems. This helps organizations maintain a secure network environment by proactively detecting and responding to potential security threats.

One of the major benefits of commercial SNMP monitoring solutions is the ease of integration with other IT management and monitoring tools. These platforms are designed to work seamlessly with a wide variety of devices and applications across different network layers, including hardware, software, and virtual environments. For example, a commercial SNMP monitoring solution might integrate with network performance management systems, IT service management (ITSM) tools, and cloud management platforms, providing a unified view of the entire IT ecosystem. This integration helps streamline workflows and ensures that administrators have the information they need in one place, making it easier to manage and optimize network performance.

Commercial SNMP monitoring solutions also tend to include extensive reporting and visualization tools that allow administrators to track network performance and generate detailed reports for auditing, compliance, and decision-making purposes. These solutions provide customizable dashboards, graphs, and charts that display key performance indicators (KPIs) for various network devices. Administrators can use these tools to quickly assess the health of the network, track performance over time, and identify potential problem areas. Reports generated by commercial solutions are often highly customizable, allowing administrators to create reports based on specific metrics, time frames, or devices. These reports are valuable for monitoring compliance with industry regulations, as well as for providing stakeholders with insight into network performance and resource utilization.

For organizations with complex network topologies or those that rely on mission-critical infrastructure, commercial SNMP monitoring solutions offer advanced automation features that reduce the need for manual intervention. Automation capabilities such as auto-discovery, configuration management, and performance tuning help streamline network management tasks, freeing up administrators to focus on more strategic initiatives. Auto-discovery, for instance, automatically detects new devices as they are added to the network and adds them to the monitoring system, ensuring that no devices are overlooked.

Similarly, configuration management features allow administrators to automate configuration changes across multiple devices, ensuring consistency and reducing the likelihood of human error.

Furthermore, commercial SNMP monitoring solutions provide comprehensive support for mobile devices, offering administrators the ability to monitor and manage network performance from anywhere at any time. Mobile apps and web-based interfaces allow administrators to receive alerts, view performance data, and take action remotely, ensuring that critical issues are addressed even when they are away from their desks. This flexibility is particularly important for large enterprises with geographically dispersed teams, as it enables administrators to maintain control of their network infrastructure regardless of location.

Commercial SNMP monitoring solutions also cater to specific industry needs, providing specialized features for verticals such as healthcare, finance, education, and manufacturing. These solutions often include industry-specific templates, compliance reporting tools, and integration capabilities that are tailored to the unique requirements of each sector. For example, healthcare organizations may require SNMP monitoring solutions that comply with HIPAA regulations and ensure the security of patient data, while financial institutions may need solutions that can handle the complexity and security demands of large-scale financial networks.

Ultimately, commercial SNMP monitoring solutions offer a comprehensive suite of features designed to help organizations manage and optimize their network infrastructure. By providing scalability, advanced features, security, and integration capabilities, these solutions help network administrators stay ahead of potential issues, ensuring the reliability and efficiency of critical network services. The combination of robust monitoring, proactive alerts, automated management, and customizable reporting makes commercial SNMP monitoring solutions an essential tool for organizations seeking to optimize their network performance while maintaining security and compliance. With these solutions, organizations can enhance their network management capabilities, reduce downtime, and improve overall business continuity.

SNMP API Integration with Other Systems

As networks grow increasingly complex, the need for seamless integration between various network management tools and systems has become a key requirement. SNMP, or Simple Network Management Protocol, is a widely adopted protocol used to monitor and manage network devices. However, in modern IT environments, network management does not occur in isolation. To fully leverage the power of SNMP for proactive monitoring, automation, and issue resolution, there is a growing need to integrate SNMP data with other enterprise systems such as IT service management (ITSM) platforms, security information and event management (SIEM) systems, cloud-based solutions, and more. By using SNMP APIs, network administrators can enable this integration, helping to centralize network management, improve operational efficiency, and provide real-time insights into system health across various platforms.

API (Application Programming Interface) integration enables different systems to communicate with one another, and in the context of SNMP, it allows the SNMP manager to interact with various software tools and databases beyond the traditional SNMP-enabled devices. Many modern SNMP monitoring solutions offer API access, allowing external systems to pull or push data from SNMP agents. This API integration empowers organizations to build customized workflows that bridge the gap between SNMP monitoring and other network management or business-critical applications. For example, an SNMP API can integrate with a ticketing system, enabling automatic creation of service tickets when a device reaches a specific threshold, such as high CPU utilization or network latency.

One of the major benefits of SNMP API integration with other systems is the centralization of monitoring data. IT operations teams often use a variety of tools for monitoring different parts of their infrastructure, such as SNMP-based monitoring tools for network devices, application performance management (APM) tools for software monitoring, and security monitoring systems to detect potential threats. By integrating SNMP with these systems via APIs, administrators can centralize the monitoring data into one interface, allowing for more efficient management. A centralized system helps operators get a holistic view of the entire infrastructure, combining network data with application, server, and security data, enabling quicker issue identification and resolution.

In addition to centralizing monitoring, API integration with SNMP helps automate various aspects of network management. For example, when an SNMP-enabled device exceeds a preconfigured threshold—such as bandwidth usage crossing a certain limit or a device going offline—an API integration can automatically trigger corrective actions. These actions can include restarting a service, scaling up cloud resources, or reconfiguring network settings. Automating these actions based on SNMP data ensures faster resolution of network issues, reduces the need for manual intervention, and improves overall system performance. Furthermore, the integration can include automated logging of these activities into the ITSM system, creating a seamless process where administrators can track, document, and report actions taken on network devices.

SNMP API integration also facilitates better collaboration between different teams within an organization. For example, when network monitoring systems detect an issue with a device or service, an SNMP API can push that alert to an incident management system, where the relevant support teams (such as the IT operations or security teams) are notified automatically. From there, the incident can be tracked through its resolution, ensuring that teams have the necessary information at each step of the process. This integration streamlines workflows and reduces the chances of communication breakdowns, allowing for faster response times and more efficient collaboration between teams.

For organizations operating in cloud environments, SNMP API integration with cloud-based systems is equally crucial. Many businesses rely on cloud services for part or all of their IT infrastructure, and ensuring that these cloud resources are properly monitored is essential for maintaining optimal performance. By integrating SNMP with cloud-based monitoring tools via APIs, administrators can extend their network monitoring capabilities to cloud services, creating a unified view that encompasses both on-premise and cloud infrastructure. For example, an API integration might allow an SNMP monitoring system to interact with AWS CloudWatch or Azure Monitor, pulling in relevant performance data from cloud-hosted devices and virtual machines. This holistic approach ensures that organizations are able to monitor and manage their entire infrastructure, regardless of whether it is on-premises or in the cloud.

In addition to performance monitoring, SNMP API integration is valuable in the realm of security. Integrating SNMP with SIEM systems allows security teams to gain deeper insights into network traffic and potential security threats. For example, if an SNMP-managed router begins to exhibit unusual behavior, such as a high volume of requests from an unrecognized IP address, an API integration could send this data to a SIEM system for further analysis. The SIEM system could then correlate this behavior with other security data, such as firewall logs or intrusion detection system alerts, helping to identify potential network attacks. By integrating SNMP data with SIEM systems through APIs, organizations can leverage advanced analytics to identify, investigate, and respond to security incidents more effectively.

Moreover, SNMP API integration can improve compliance reporting and auditing processes. Many industries are subject to strict regulations that require organizations to maintain detailed logs of network activities and security events. By using SNMP APIs to collect data from various network devices and feeding this data into centralized compliance platforms, administrators can ensure that they are meeting regulatory requirements. SNMP data can provide insights into the health of devices, the performance of critical systems, and any anomalies or issues that need to be addressed. By integrating SNMP data with compliance management platforms via APIs, organizations can automate the process of data collection, reporting, and auditing, reducing the risk of non-compliance and streamlining the overall process.

API integration can also help with advanced analytics and machine learning (ML) applications. With more organizations relying on big data and AI to optimize their IT infrastructure, SNMP APIs can feed valuable performance metrics into analytics platforms for deeper analysis. This data can be used to predict network performance trends, detect potential failures before they occur, and optimize resource allocation. Machine learning algorithms can analyze historical SNMP data to identify patterns and predict future performance issues, helping administrators proactively address problems before they impact the organization. This type of predictive maintenance is especially useful in large-scale environments, where the number of devices and systems being monitored can make it difficult to anticipate issues manually.

The growing complexity of modern networks demands that SNMP data be integrated with a variety of other management systems, each serving a distinct purpose. By leveraging SNMP APIs, organizations can bridge the gap between these systems, allowing for the seamless exchange of data and enabling a more unified approach to network management. Whether it's automating network performance optimization, improving security monitoring, ensuring compliance, or enhancing the collaboration between teams, SNMP API integration plays a key role in maximizing the value of SNMP data. By integrating SNMP with other systems through APIs, organizations can improve their overall network management capabilities, resulting in more efficient, secure, and optimized network operations.

SNMP Troubleshooting Techniques

Network administrators often encounter a variety of challenges when working with SNMP (Simple Network Management Protocol), a protocol that is widely used for monitoring and managing network devices. The distributed nature of SNMP, which involves numerous devices and network segments, can lead to connectivity issues, misconfigurations, or security concerns that can interfere with its functionality. Troubleshooting SNMP requires a methodical approach to identify and resolve problems related to SNMP agents, managers, devices, network infrastructure, and configuration settings. Whether it's a connectivity issue, incorrect data reporting, or a failure to respond to SNMP queries, effective troubleshooting techniques can help restore normal operation and ensure that the network is being monitored effectively.

One of the first steps in SNMP troubleshooting is ensuring that SNMP is enabled and properly configured on both the SNMP agents (the network devices being monitored) and the SNMP manager (the system querying the devices). Administrators should begin by confirming that SNMP is enabled on the devices in question and that the correct SNMP version is being used. SNMP has evolved through multiple versions, each with different levels of security. SNMPv1 and SNMPv2c, for example, rely on community strings for authentication and are less secure than SNMPv3, which offers stronger security through authentication and encryption. Administrators must verify that the devices are running the correct version of SNMP and that any necessary community strings or authentication credentials are correctly configured.

Once it is confirmed that SNMP is enabled, administrators should check for network connectivity issues. The most common reason for SNMP failures is simple network connectivity problems between the SNMP manager and the SNMP agents. Administrators should use basic network troubleshooting tools such as ping or traceroute to confirm that the SNMP manager can reach the target devices. If there are issues with network connectivity, it could be due to misconfigured network devices, firewalls blocking SNMP traffic, or routing issues that prevent the manager from reaching the SNMP agent. In particular, firewalls may block UDP traffic on the ports used by SNMP (typically port 161 for queries and port 162 for traps), so it's essential to ensure that these ports are open and that no other network security devices are interfering with SNMP traffic.

Another critical area to check during SNMP troubleshooting is the access control settings on the devices. SNMP often uses community strings for authentication, especially in SNMPv1 and SNMPv2c. These community strings are essentially passwords that allow the SNMP manager to access the MIB (Management Information Base) on a device. If the community strings are misconfigured or do not match between the manager and the agent, SNMP queries will fail. This is a common issue when there are configuration errors or if default community strings (such as "public" or "private") are used. In such cases, changing community strings to unique, complex values and ensuring that the same community string is configured on both the manager and agent can resolve the problem.

For devices running SNMPv3, troubleshooting should also include verifying the authentication and encryption settings. SNMPv3 provides higher security by using user-based authentication and encryption to protect SNMP traffic. If the credentials or encryption settings are incorrect, SNMP queries will not work. Administrators should check that the correct user credentials are configured on both the SNMP manager and the agent, ensuring that the authentication method (e.g., SHA or MD5) and encryption (e.g., DES or AES) are consistent between the two. Additionally, it's important to verify that the SNMP engine IDs are properly configured, as mismatches in engine IDs can lead to authentication failures.

One effective troubleshooting tool in SNMP troubleshooting is SNMPwalk. SNMPwalk allows administrators to query a device for its entire set of MIB objects, providing a comprehensive view of the data available through SNMP. By using SNMPwalk, administrators can verify if the device is responding correctly to SNMP queries and identify which MIB objects are accessible. If SNMPwalk fails to return data, it may indicate a configuration problem with the device, such as an incorrect community string or an issue with the SNMP agent. Administrators can also use SNMPget to check individual MIB objects to further isolate the issue.

If SNMP traps are not being received by the SNMP manager, it may indicate a problem with the trap configuration or network communication. SNMP traps are used by devices to send alerts or notifications about critical events, such as hardware failures, interface status changes, or threshold breaches. In this case, administrators should check that the SNMP trap destination is correctly configured on the device and that the IP address of the SNMP manager is properly specified. Additionally, it is important to verify that the device is capable of sending traps, as some devices may need specific configurations or firmware updates to support this feature. If firewalls or network devices are blocking SNMP trap traffic, this should also be addressed to ensure the trap messages can reach the monitoring system.

In addition to these steps, checking the device's MIB and SNMP agent logs is also essential. The MIB contains the definitions of all the objects that can be monitored on a device, and if there are issues with SNMP data collection, the MIB may provide valuable clues. Many SNMP agents also generate log files that can indicate the source of problems, such as failed authentication attempts, unreachable devices, or errors in processing SNMP requests. These logs can often provide useful diagnostic information that can help pinpoint the root cause of SNMP failures.

Furthermore, network administrators should consider the impact of SNMP polling frequency on system performance. Excessive polling of SNMP devices can put unnecessary strain on network resources and devices, potentially leading to performance degradation. If SNMP queries are set too frequently or if the network is heavily loaded with monitoring traffic, it can cause delays or missed responses. Adjusting the polling intervals to a reasonable frequency and ensuring that network resources are not overwhelmed can help resolve issues related to SNMP performance.

Another important consideration during SNMP troubleshooting is ensuring that the network topology is correctly represented in the SNMP management platform. In large networks, devices may be added, moved, or removed, and these changes may not be reflected in the SNMP manager's configuration. It's important to regularly update the management platform with the latest network topology to ensure that all devices are being monitored correctly. This can be done through SNMP discovery tools or by manually adding new devices to the monitoring system.

Finally, for complex network environments, administrators should leverage network monitoring systems that provide detailed diagnostic tools for SNMP troubleshooting. Tools such as Wireshark, which is a network protocol analyzer, can capture SNMP traffic between the manager and agent, allowing administrators to see the raw SNMP requests and responses. Analyzing this traffic can help identify where the issue lies, whether it is with the SNMP query, the response, or network-related problems.

SNMP troubleshooting requires a systematic approach, starting with confirming that SNMP is enabled, ensuring proper configuration, and diagnosing network connectivity issues. Tools like SNMPwalk, SNMPget, and network protocol analyzers such as Wireshark can assist administrators in identifying and resolving issues. By examining logs, validating configurations, and considering factors such as SNMP polling frequency and device performance, administrators can quickly isolate and fix SNMP-related problems, ensuring that network management remains effective and reliable.

SNMP in Incident Response

In the modern networked world, incidents that compromise the availability, integrity, and confidentiality of network infrastructure can occur unexpectedly, often requiring immediate attention to prevent significant disruptions. Network monitoring protocols such as SNMP (Simple Network Management Protocol) play a crucial role in incident response by providing real-time visibility into the status and health of network devices, systems, and services. When integrated into a network's incident response strategy, SNMP enables administrators to identify, assess, and mitigate the impact of incidents quickly and effectively. It acts as an early warning system, delivering valuable information about performance issues, security breaches, or operational failures.

The ability of SNMP to support real-time monitoring is particularly useful during incident response. As part of the proactive measures employed in network security, SNMP allows administrators to track and record performance data, enabling the early detection of abnormal activity that might indicate a security breach or failure in network components. For example, if a router or server experiences a sudden spike in CPU usage or network traffic, SNMP can alert administrators to the anomaly before it escalates into a full-blown incident. SNMP data, when monitored in real-time, can provide insights into which devices or services are affected and help prioritize response efforts based on the severity of the incident.

In the context of incident response, SNMP traps are a particularly valuable feature. SNMP traps are unsolicited messages sent by devices to notify SNMP managers of specific events, such as hardware failures, security violations, or threshold breaches. Unlike SNMP polls, which require the SNMP manager to query devices for information, traps provide immediate notifications, allowing network administrators to respond to incidents as soon as they occur. This real-time alerting system ensures that administrators are promptly informed about critical events, enabling them to take quick action to minimize downtime, limit damage, and resolve issues before they worsen. For example, a trap might be sent when a network switch detects an unauthorized device attempting to connect, allowing security teams to block the device or investigate the intrusion attempt before it can spread further.

Another aspect of SNMP's usefulness in incident response lies in its integration with broader network monitoring and security systems. SNMP-enabled devices, such as firewalls, routers, and intrusion detection systems (IDS), can be monitored using SNMP to gather data about network traffic patterns, device status, and security-related events. When integrated with Security Information and Event Management (SIEM) systems, SNMP data can be correlated with logs from other security devices, helping to provide a more comprehensive view of the incident. By aggregating data from multiple sources, such as firewalls, routers, and switches, administrators can identify patterns of behavior that might indicate a coordinated attack, such as a DDoS (Distributed Denial of Service) attack, and respond accordingly.

SNMP also plays an important role in diagnosing and troubleshooting network issues during an incident. When a failure occurs, SNMP allows administrators to gather real-time statistics and error messages from network devices, providing essential context for understanding the root cause of the issue. For instance, if a server becomes unresponsive, SNMP can provide metrics such as CPU usage, memory utilization, and network performance, allowing administrators to determine whether the issue is due to resource exhaustion, hardware failure, or network congestion. Additionally, SNMP can help identify misconfigured devices, faulty connections, or other issues that could be contributing to the incident. By enabling administrators to quickly pinpoint the source of the problem, SNMP accelerates the troubleshooting process and facilitates faster incident resolution.

During an incident, it is essential to have accurate and up-to-date information about the affected devices and their status. SNMP provides the capability to query and retrieve device configuration details, helping administrators understand the current state of the network and the devices involved in the incident. For example, if an attacker gains access to a network switch, SNMP can be used to determine the current configuration settings, including the list of connected devices, VLAN configurations, and interface status. By retrieving this information, administrators can identify any unauthorized changes made by the attacker and take steps to restore the network to its secure state.

Another key benefit of using SNMP in incident response is its ability to support automation and orchestration. In large networks, manual intervention may not be feasible for every incident. By integrating SNMP monitoring with automation platforms, organizations can automate response actions based on predefined conditions. For example, if an SNMP trap is triggered indicating a critical network device is down, an automation platform could initiate a pre-configured workflow to restart the device, reroute traffic, or escalate the incident to the appropriate personnel. Automating routine tasks not only accelerates response times but also reduces the risk of human error, ensuring that critical steps are consistently taken during incidents.

SNMP is also valuable for post-incident analysis and reporting. After an incident has been resolved, it is essential to understand what happened, what caused the disruption, and how to prevent similar incidents in the future. SNMP data, particularly performance metrics and logs from devices involved in the incident, can provide insights into the sequence of events that led to the issue. By reviewing SNMP logs and analyzing historical data, administrators can identify trends, recurring problems, and vulnerabilities that may have contributed to the incident. This post-mortem analysis is critical for improving network resilience and refining incident response plans to better address similar challenges in the future.

Furthermore, SNMP allows for continuous monitoring even after an incident has been resolved. By maintaining a constant flow of SNMP data, administrators can ensure that network performance remains stable and that no lingering issues are overlooked. Ongoing monitoring also helps verify that the corrective actions taken during the incident have been effective, ensuring that devices are functioning optimally and that the network remains secure. For example, if a vulnerability was identified during the incident and patched, SNMP monitoring can be used to confirm that the patch was successfully applied and that no new security issues have emerged.

While SNMP is a powerful tool for incident response, it is essential to ensure that it is configured securely to prevent misuse. SNMPv1 and SNMPv2c, for example, transmit data in plaintext, making them vulnerable to interception and exploitation. To ensure that SNMP does not become a potential attack vector, organizations should adopt SNMPv3, which offers enhanced security features such as encryption, authentication, and data integrity. Properly configuring SNMP access control, using strong community strings or user credentials, and segmenting SNMP traffic from other network traffic are also critical measures to protect SNMP from unauthorized access.

In the broader context of incident response, SNMP serves as a critical component for monitoring, detecting, and mitigating incidents in real-time. Its ability to provide valuable data on the health and status of network devices enables administrators to quickly detect anomalies, troubleshoot problems, and take corrective actions before issues escalate. By integrating SNMP into a comprehensive incident response strategy, organizations can improve their ability to respond to network incidents and reduce the time and resources required to resolve them.

Future Trends in SNMP and Network Management

As networks become more complex, and the demand for seamless, efficient, and secure communication grows, the role of SNMP (Simple Network Management Protocol) in network management is evolving. The continuous growth in internet-connected devices, increased reliance on cloud services, and the rise of software-defined networking (SDN) and the Internet of Things (IoT) are reshaping the landscape of network management. SNMP has long been a cornerstone of network monitoring, but as technological advancements push the boundaries of what networks can do, the future of SNMP and network management is poised for significant transformation. Several key trends are emerging in SNMP and network management, reflecting the changing needs of businesses and the advancements in networking technology.

One of the most significant trends in SNMP and network management is the increasing integration of artificial intelligence (AI) and machine learning (ML) into network monitoring platforms. AI and ML can revolutionize how networks are managed by providing deep insights into network behavior, enabling predictive maintenance, and automating troubleshooting. Traditional SNMP monitoring tools typically rely on fixed thresholds to trigger alerts when network devices exceed certain performance metrics. However, these static thresholds can often lead to either missed opportunities for early intervention or an overwhelming number of false alarms. AI and ML algorithms can analyze vast amounts of SNMP data to detect anomalies and predict issues before they happen, allowing for more intelligent network management. For example, AI could recognize patterns in SNMP data that indicate a potential failure or security breach, even before the issue becomes critical. This predictive capability will allow network administrators to address problems proactively, reducing downtime and improving network reliability.

Another trend gaining momentum in the future of SNMP and network management is the increasing importance of automation. The complexity and scale of modern networks require automation to efficiently manage the growing number of networked devices. SNMP itself is already a highly automated protocol for querying and monitoring devices, but the next step is the integration of SNMP into fully automated network management workflows. With network automation, SNMP can be used not only to monitor the network but also to trigger automated responses to certain conditions. For instance, if an SNMP-enabled device experiences high latency, an automated system might reconfigure network routes to bypass the affected device or initiate a failover process. This level of automation reduces the need for manual intervention, speeds up response times, and improves network resilience. The adoption of automation in SNMP management will also support software-defined networking (SDN), where network resources are dynamically allocated based on real-time performance data, often derived from SNMP queries.

The rise of cloud computing is another major influence on the future of SNMP and network management. As more organizations move their workloads to the cloud, the complexity of monitoring and managing hybrid networks – those that span on-premises data centers and cloud environments – increases. SNMP will need to evolve to handle this new reality, especially with the increasing use of cloud-native technologies such as microservices and containers. In a cloud-based environment, SNMP monitoring must extend beyond traditional network devices to include virtualized environments, such as cloud servers, storage solutions, and application services. The cloud introduces challenges related to scalability, resource allocation, and security, which will require new approaches to network management. Future SNMP solutions will likely integrate more closely with cloud management platforms, providing network administrators with a unified view of both on-premises and cloud infrastructure. SNMP will continue to be an important part of this multi-cloud management model, helping administrators track device performance, service availability, and network health across various environments.

In tandem with cloud computing, the growth of IoT devices is reshaping the landscape of network management. The proliferation of IoT devices, which often lack traditional management interfaces, presents unique challenges for network administrators. Many IoT devices are lightweight and specialized, making them difficult to manage with traditional SNMP tools. However, as IoT continues to expand across industries such as manufacturing, healthcare, and smart cities, SNMP will need to evolve to support a larger variety of device types and use cases. Future SNMP solutions will likely need to provide more flexible management capabilities for IoT devices, enabling administrators to monitor their performance, security, and health without introducing significant overhead. This could include enhanced SNMP support for low-power, low-bandwidth IoT devices, as well as the development of new standards that allow for the integration of IoT data into existing network management platforms.

Another future trend is the development of more secure SNMP protocols. While SNMPv3 introduced security features such as encryption and authentication, the increasing sophistication of cyber threats calls for continuous improvements in network security. Future versions of SNMP will likely incorporate even stronger security mechanisms to protect against evolving threats. One area of focus will be the improvement of encryption algorithms to ensure that sensitive network data is protected from interception. Additionally, tighter integration with network security tools, such as intrusion detection systems (IDS) and security information and event management (SIEM) systems, will provide a more comprehensive approach to network monitoring and incident response. By combining SNMP with advanced security tools, organizations can enhance their ability to detect and mitigate threats in real-time.

The increasing need for real-time visibility into network performance and the demand for continuous monitoring also suggests that SNMP management will become more integrated with real-time analytics platforms. Network administrators will require access to more dynamic data from SNMP-managed devices, particularly as the demand for instantaneous performance metrics grows. The future of SNMP will likely see closer integration with big data analytics platforms, enabling organizations to extract valuable insights from the massive volumes of data generated by network devices. By integrating SNMP with advanced analytics and visualization tools, network administrators will be able to make data-driven decisions more quickly and optimize network performance in real-time.

In line with the growing emphasis on data-driven network management, future SNMP solutions will likely evolve to provide more granular insights into network behavior. Enhanced SNMP tools will support deeper levels of data analysis, allowing administrators to not only monitor device health but also understand the underlying causes of performance issues. For example, future SNMP tools might use machine learning algorithms to detect patterns of behavior that precede network failures, enabling administrators to take preemptive action. This deeper level of insight will enable organizations to optimize their networks more effectively and reduce the likelihood of service interruptions.

As organizations increasingly adopt agile and DevOps methodologies, SNMP monitoring will also evolve to support more rapid deployment and configuration of network monitoring solutions. Future SNMP management tools will likely be designed to integrate seamlessly into DevOps pipelines, providing automated network monitoring as part of continuous integration and continuous deployment (CI/CD) workflows. This will enable network administrators to deploy new SNMP configurations quickly and efficiently, reducing the time to detect and resolve network issues.

In the future, SNMP will continue to be a critical component of network management, but it will need to adapt to the changing technological landscape. The integration of AI, machine learning, automation, and advanced security features will drive the evolution of SNMP and network management platforms. As cloud computing, IoT, and SDN continue to reshape how networks are designed and managed, SNMP will evolve to meet the demands of a more dynamic, interconnected, and data-driven network environment. These changes will empower network administrators to manage complex infrastructures more effectively, ensuring that network performance remains optimal and security risks are minimized in an increasingly connected world.

Comparing SNMP with Modern Alternatives

As the network landscape continues to evolve, so too do the tools and protocols used to monitor, manage, and secure networks. For many years, Simple Network Management Protocol (SNMP) has been the go-to solution for network management, providing a standardized way for administrators to monitor devices, gather performance metrics, and detect issues in real-time. However, with the rapid advancement of networking technologies and the increasing complexity of modern networks, several alternative monitoring and management solutions have emerged. These alternatives are often designed to address the limitations of SNMP and provide additional capabilities that are better suited to the needs of today's network environments. While SNMP continues to play an important role, it is essential to compare it with these modern alternatives to understand their respective strengths and weaknesses and determine the most suitable solution for a given network.

One of the primary limitations of SNMP is its relatively simple, static nature. Originally designed in the 1980s, SNMP was created to monitor devices and collect basic performance metrics, such as CPU load, memory usage, and network interface statistics. Over the years, SNMP has evolved to support more advanced features, especially in SNMPv3, which includes improvements like security enhancements through encryption and authentication. However, despite these advancements, SNMP remains a relatively basic protocol that requires manual configuration, lacks deep analytics capabilities, and is limited in terms of automation. This has led to the development of more modern alternatives, such as RESTful APIs, NETCONF, and other network monitoring systems, which provide greater flexibility, scalability, and real-time insights.

One significant alternative to SNMP is the use of RESTful APIs. REST (Representational State Transfer) has become the standard for web-based communication, particularly in cloud computing and modern applications. RESTful APIs are widely used to interface with cloud services, virtual machines, and software-defined networking (SDN) components. Unlike SNMP, which requires dedicated agents to be installed on each monitored device, RESTful APIs allow for easy integration with existing systems and can be used to collect data from a variety of devices and services, including cloud platforms and virtualized environments. The advantage of RESTful APIs is their flexibility and ease of use. They allow network administrators to query data from devices in real-time using standard HTTP methods such as GET, POST, PUT, and DELETE. Additionally, RESTful APIs are typically easier to configure and integrate with modern monitoring platforms than SNMP, making them an attractive alternative for managing cloud-based and software-defined infrastructures.

Another modern alternative to SNMP is NETCONF, a network configuration protocol that offers more advanced capabilities than SNMP, especially when it comes to network automation and configuration management. NETCONF was developed to address the need for a more sophisticated, scalable protocol capable of managing the configurations of complex networks. Unlike SNMP, which is primarily focused on monitoring, NETCONF allows administrators to perform both configuration and monitoring tasks. It supports features such as transactional operations, data validation, and the ability to modify configurations dynamically, making it an ideal solution for managing modern, programmable networks. NETCONF is especially beneficial in environments where automation and orchestration are essential, such as in SDN or large-scale data centers. It provides a structured, XML-based interface that allows for the automated management of network devices, including routers, switches, and firewalls, and can be used to push configuration changes across an entire network in a consistent manner.

In addition to RESTful APIs and NETCONF, newer monitoring systems such as Prometheus and Grafana have gained popularity in the network monitoring space. Prometheus is an open-source monitoring and alerting toolkit designed for reliability and scalability. It is particularly useful for monitoring dynamic, containerized environments like Kubernetes, where traditional monitoring tools like SNMP struggle to provide the level of detail and flexibility required. Prometheus uses a pull-based model, where it scrapes data from various endpoints at regular intervals, collecting performance metrics from servers, applications, and network devices. It is highly flexible, allowing users to define custom metrics and alerting rules based on real-time data. Grafana is often used alongside Prometheus for visualization, enabling network administrators to create interactive dashboards and graphs that display data from various sources in a unified interface. Together, Prometheus and Grafana provide a modern, cloud-native alternative to SNMP that offers greater scalability, detailed performance insights, and sophisticated alerting capabilities.

While SNMP remains a valuable tool for many network management tasks, these modern alternatives offer several advantages. One of the most significant benefits of RESTful APIs, NETCONF, and systems like Prometheus is their ability to integrate seamlessly with a wide variety of platforms and services. Unlike SNMP, which is often limited to traditional hardware devices and network components, modern alternatives support hybrid environments that include cloud-based services, virtual machines, containers, and SDN-based networks. As more organizations migrate to cloud environments and adopt containerized applications, these alternatives provide the necessary flexibility to monitor and manage a diverse set of devices and services.

Another advantage of modern alternatives is their ability to provide more granular, real-time insights into network performance. While SNMP is capable of monitoring basic performance metrics such as interface status and device availability, newer solutions like Prometheus allow for deep metrics collection and advanced analytics. Prometheus, for example, can track detailed performance metrics at the application level, such as request latency, error rates, and throughput, which are not typically available with SNMP. This level of detail enables administrators to gain a deeper understanding of their network's health, identify performance bottlenecks, and troubleshoot issues more effectively.

Furthermore, modern alternatives often offer better scalability and automation capabilities compared to SNMP. In large, complex networks, manually configuring and managing SNMP devices can become cumbersome and error-prone. Tools like NETCONF and Prometheus enable network administrators to automate many aspects of network management, from configuration changes to data collection and alerting. NETCONF, with its support for transaction-based operations and configuration validation, is particularly well-suited for large-scale automation, allowing for consistent, reliable management of network devices across an entire infrastructure. This level of automation is increasingly important as networks grow in size and complexity, especially in environments such as data centers or cloud-based infrastructures, where traditional SNMP monitoring may not be sufficient.

While these modern alternatives offer many advantages over SNMP, it is important to recognize that SNMP still holds value in certain contexts. SNMP remains widely supported across a vast array of devices, from network routers and switches to printers and security cameras. It is often easier to deploy and configure in environments where devices are standardized and do not require the sophisticated features provided by newer protocols. Moreover, SNMP's simplicity and well-established presence in network management make it a reliable choice for smaller or more traditional networks that do not require the advanced capabilities offered by alternatives like NETCONF or Prometheus.

In sum, while SNMP remains a staple in network management, its limitations in terms of scalability, flexibility, and automation are becoming more apparent as networks evolve. Modern alternatives, including RESTful APIs, NETCONF, and tools like Prometheus and

Grafana, offer advanced features that better meet the needs of today's dynamic, cloud-native, and software-defined environments. These alternatives provide deeper insights into network performance, greater integration with diverse platforms, and enhanced automation capabilities, making them powerful options for managing complex networks. However, SNMP will continue to be relevant in certain contexts, particularly in simpler, more standardized environments where its simplicity and wide device support are key advantages.

Conclusion: The Role of SNMP in Secure Network Operations

The Simple Network Management Protocol (SNMP) has long been a cornerstone of network monitoring and management, providing network administrators with the tools necessary to ensure the health, security, and performance of their network infrastructure. As networks grow in complexity and size, the role of SNMP becomes even more critical, offering administrators the ability to monitor a wide range of devices and systems, from traditional routers and switches to cloud services and IoT devices. Despite the emergence of new technologies and protocols, SNMP remains an essential protocol for secure network operations. When used correctly and securely, SNMP offers a powerful means to keep networks running smoothly, detect anomalies, and respond to issues before they affect the organization's business operations.

SNMP's role in network security has evolved over time. Initially, SNMP was a simple protocol that allowed administrators to retrieve data from network devices. However, with the rise in security threats, SNMP has adapted, especially with the introduction of SNMPv3, which brought essential security features such as authentication, encryption, and message integrity. These enhancements significantly mitigated the risks associated with SNMP communication, addressing weaknesses that existed in earlier versions. SNMPv3 is now the standard for secure SNMP communication, enabling organizations to securely manage their devices and gather critical performance data without exposing themselves to unnecessary security risks. This is particularly important in an age where network breaches and cyber-attacks are becoming more sophisticated and frequent.

The primary role of SNMP in secure network operations lies in its ability to provide real-time visibility into the status of network devices and infrastructure. By continuously monitoring devices such as routers, switches, firewalls, and servers, SNMP enables administrators to track performance metrics such as CPU usage, memory utilization, bandwidth consumption, and device availability. This continuous monitoring is essential for identifying potential issues that could lead to network outages, security vulnerabilities, or performance degradation. When configured properly, SNMP allows for the proactive identification of these issues, allowing administrators to take corrective action before problems escalate. This proactive approach not only ensures optimal performance but also strengthens the security posture of the network by identifying unusual behavior or vulnerabilities early.

The ability to gather real-time data from SNMP-enabled devices also enables network administrators to respond quickly to security incidents. SNMP traps, which are notifications sent by devices when certain events or conditions occur, provide an efficient means for administrators to be alerted to critical incidents as they happen. For example, an SNMP trap can be configured to notify administrators if a device goes offline, if there is a significant increase in network traffic, or if a device reports a hardware failure. These real-time alerts allow for immediate intervention, reducing the risk of extended downtime or more severe security breaches. When integrated with other security tools, such as intrusion detection systems (IDS) or security information and event management (SIEM) systems, SNMP provides a comprehensive approach to network security, enabling organizations to quickly detect and respond to threats.

In secure network operations, access control and proper configuration of SNMP are key components in ensuring that only authorized personnel can access network management data. The security of SNMP heavily depends on the strength of the authentication and encryption settings. SNMPv3, with its built-in support for strong authentication and encryption, offers significant protection against unauthorized access and data interception. However, even with SNMPv3, the configuration must be managed carefully to avoid common mistakes that could leave the network vulnerable. Administrators must ensure that SNMP community strings are unique, that SNMP access is restricted to authorized IP addresses, and that encrypted communication is used to protect sensitive data. Failure to properly secure SNMP communications can expose an organization to significant security risks, including unauthorized monitoring and device manipulation.

In addition to its monitoring and alerting capabilities, SNMP plays a crucial role in network configuration and management. Many network devices support SNMP-based configuration management, enabling administrators to make real-time changes to device settings, including adjusting parameters, enabling or disabling interfaces, or implementing security policies. For example, administrators can use SNMP to configure access control lists (ACLs) on routers or firewalls, helping to secure the network and control traffic flow. When used in conjunction with configuration management tools and automation, SNMP allows for the efficient deployment of configuration changes across multiple devices, ensuring consistency and reducing the risk of misconfigurations that could leave the network exposed to vulnerabilities.

However, as networks continue to grow in size and complexity, SNMP by itself may no longer be sufficient to meet the demands of modern network environments. The rise of cloud computing, software-defined networking (SDN), and the Internet of Things (IoT) has introduced new challenges for network management. These technologies often require more granular monitoring and real-time visibility into not only network devices but also applications, virtualized environments, and cloud-based services. While SNMP can still play a role in monitoring these environments, it needs to be integrated with more modern monitoring tools and protocols to provide a complete view of the network's health and security. Tools such as RESTful APIs, NETCONF, and monitoring solutions like Prometheus and Grafana are increasingly being used in conjunction with SNMP to provide deeper insights, better scalability, and more automation.

One of the most pressing concerns in network security today is the protection of sensitive data. With the increasing amount of personal and financial information being transmitted over networks, ensuring the confidentiality and integrity of data is paramount. SNMP, when properly secured, helps ensure that sensitive network data is not exposed to unauthorized access or tampering. This is particularly important in industries like finance, healthcare, and government, where regulatory requirements for data protection are stringent. SNMP's ability to encrypt communications and authenticate users helps protect data from unauthorized access, ensuring that only legitimate network administrators can view and manage sensitive network configurations and performance data.

The integration of SNMP with other network security tools further enhances its effectiveness in securing network operations. By integrating SNMP with firewalls, intrusion detection/prevention systems, and SIEM solutions, administrators can gain a more comprehensive view of network activity and security events. For example, SNMP traps can be used to send alerts about abnormal traffic patterns, which can then be analyzed by the SIEM system for potential threats. This integration enables organizations to correlate data from multiple sources and respond to incidents more effectively, improving the overall security posture of the network.

As network management continues to evolve, SNMP will remain a key player in ensuring the stability, security, and performance of network infrastructure. While it may not be the most advanced or feature-rich solution available today, SNMP's simplicity, scalability, and long-standing reliability ensure that it will continue to play an important role in secure network operations. By leveraging SNMP alongside modern technologies and adhering to best practices for security and configuration management, organizations can maintain a secure, efficient, and resilient network environment.

www.ingramcontent.com/pod-product-compliance
Lightning Source LLC
La Vergne TN
LVHW051234050326
832903LV00028B/2404